The Way of the Shepherd

The Way of the Shepherd

Dr. Kevin Leman
William Pentak

OMF Literature Inc.
Manila, Philippines

The Way of the Shepherd

All Scripture quotations, unless otherwise indicated, are taken from the Holy Bible: New International Version®. *NIV®. Copyright © 1973, 1978, 1984 by International Bible Society. Used by permission of Zondervan. All rights reserved.*

Interior design by Beth Shagene

Published (2005) in the Philippines by
OMF Literature Inc.
776 Boni Avenue
Mandaluyong City, Metro Manila
www.OMFLit.com

This edition issued by special arrangement with
ZONDERVAN
WWW.ZONDERVAN.COM
Grand Rapids, Michigan, USA

Reprinted — 2005 (twice), 2006, 2007 (four times), 2008 (twice), 2009

ISBN 978-971-511-878-1

Printed in the Philippines

To the best shepherds we know,
Jodie and Sande

and to William's little flock,
Marshall and Anna

ACKNOWLEDGMENTS:

Thanks to our insightful, perfectionistic, and very helpful editor, John Sloan, for his invaluable assistance.

Contents

The Interview

In my lowly role as cub reporter, I had just returned from covering my third ribbon-cutting ceremony of the week. That's when I found the pink While You Were Out slip, with Christina Nickel's name on it. This book is the result of her unexpected call to the *Texas Star*'s newsroom.

Hungry to impress my editor, I had called Christina three weeks earlier, requesting an interview with the reclusive Theodore McBride, the most respected business leader in America. He had led General Technologies to seventeen years of unprecedented success during his ongoing reign as CEO.

Bracing myself for a letdown, I dialed Christina's number. She got right to the point. "Mr. Pentak," she said, "Mr. McBride asked me to return your call."

"Yes," I said, holding my breath.

"He's agreed to do the interview."

I was stunned.

On the day of the interview, I arrived a little early at General Technologies' world headquarters so I could get the lay of the land. Two things immediately struck me. First, I couldn't help but notice the dynamic atmosphere. You could sense the energy that employees radiated as they scurried throughout the building. Second, General Technologies obviously worked hard at making its employees feel valued. From the lobby and health club to the credit union and employee food court, even on the flat-screen monitors in the elevators, appeared the words "General Technologies: Our People Are Our Greatest Competitive Advantage."

I need to come work here, I caught myself thinking on my trip to the fortieth floor. *Must be nice to work in a place where you don't feel like a cog in a wheel.*

Moments later I found myself standing in the anteroom of Theodore McBride's office, talking to Christina Nickel. "Hello, Mr. Pentak," she said. "Mr. McBride is expecting you. He's wrapping up an overseas conference call and will be available shortly."

"No problem," I said, taking the opportunity to probe. "Tell me, how long have you worked for Mr. McBride?"

She turned and smiled. "Fourteen years," she answered.

"I take it you must like working for him to stay so long."

"Mr. McBride is the best person I've ever worked for," she declared.

"Why's that?" I asked.

At that moment she noticed that McBride's extension light had gone off on her phone console. "He's ready. Right this way." While reaching for McBride's door, she answered my question. "He expects the best from us, and we give it to him because we know he's giving his best to us in return."

The door swung open, and I found myself face-to-face with the legendary Theodore McBride, looking for all the world like someone's grandfather. He surprised me by speaking first.

"It's a pleasure to meet you, Mr. Pentak," he said, firmly clasping my hand in both of his. "I'm Ted McBride." Suddenly I felt like I was nine years old and back in short pants. *I can't believe I'm this nervous,* I thought.

After several minutes of small talk, however, the Old Man had me completely at ease. He had an engaging personality and listened intently to everything I said. Finally, I asked the question that had kept me up nearly the entire night.

"Tell me," I said, "I've been dying to know—"

"Why I chose you to do the interview?" he interrupted.

"Yes," I nodded, "and why now?"

"Because you're green and inexperienced and haven't yet been tainted with arrogance. In terms of why now, at the moment you don't need to know. You just need to know that I have my reasons."

He noted the puckered expression on my face and continued. "Look, don't take that personally. I get a hundred requests a year to do what we're going to do here today. All of them come from seasoned business broadcast and media journalists who already 'know' all the answers. They get on the nightly news and pontificate with absolute certainty about what the market is going to do and why. The only problem is, one will say with absolute certainty that the market is going to go up, while another will say with equal assurance that it's going down. These are the same people who have reported on my company for years.

"One time, one of your more sensational competitors wrote, after I had cashed in a sizeable portion of my stock options, that I had insider information that our company was about to experience a severe decline in earnings. He accused me of cashing out ahead of the public and suggested that I should be investigated by the SEC. Everyone else picked it up because it was 'news.' The only problem was the decline in earnings never came; I had cashed out to pay for my daughter's wedding, nothing more. I chose you, Mr. Pentak, because you don't write that way. There's an honesty about your writing. What's more, you're still young and idealistic enough to be teachable. I'm not going to hand over the seven greatest management principles to anyone who already has all the answers."

"The seven greatest management principles?" I mumbled, wondering if the interview was about to turn into something more than I had planned.

"Yes. It's no surprise General Technologies has been the number one company to work for in America for much of the last decade. There's a spirit of teamwork here that isn't found in most companies. That didn't happen by accident."

"It happened because of the seven principles?" I asked.

"Absolutely. The best part is you don't have to be a company of fifty thousand to see them work. They'll work in any setting, for anyone who knows and acts upon them. It doesn't matter if you're a sales manager for a pharmaceutical giant, a manager of a small fast-food franchise, or the director of a Sunday school department. It doesn't matter, because people are the same wherever you go. You just have to know what the principles are and follow them."

"How did you come up with them?" I inquired.

"I didn't," he replied flatly. He rose from his chair and walked over to the window. "They were handed down to me. They were given to me by the greatest man, outside of my father, that I ever knew. He handed them down to me when I wasn't much older than you are." He peered out the window, pausing just long enough for effect, then added, "Now . . . I'm going to hand them down to you."

I quickly put away my list of prepared questions and whipped out my blank notepad.

CHAPTER 1

KNOW THE CONDITION OF YOUR FLOCK

I was an MBA student about to graduate from the University of Texas at Austin," McBride continued. "The last semester all of us were exhilarated that we had actually survived the program. Our professors threw so much information at us so quickly, we used to joke it was like trying to take a sip from a fire hydrant. But despite feeling ecstatic, we also felt anxious to find work and therefore busied ourselves with recruitment interviews on the UT campus. Finally the day arrived that I had been dreaming of. I landed a position with General Technologies. I was thrilled to no end . . . and terrified."

"What terrified you?" I asked.

"I was hired as a manager in the financial operations division, where I would supervise nine people."

"So you worried you weren't up to the job?"

"Yes and no. I wasn't afraid of working in the finance department; it was the idea of supervising nine people that scared me to death." McBride turned as if to look at something far away. He shook his head slowly. "When I look back now," he continued, "well . . . it makes me laugh. I was a cocky MBA with all the answers, but I didn't have a clue where to start when it came to managing people."

"So what did you do?" I probed.

"I went to see one of my professors, Dr. Jack Neumann. He had taught one of our courses in the MBA program. He was also my mentor. The day I landed the General Technologies job I couldn't wait to tell him the good news. I also wanted to ask for his help."

"And he was the one who taught you the seven principles?"

"Exactly."

And so McBride sat down and began to tell a story that at times sounded more like fiction than fact. But according to him, what he learned from Dr. Neumann had unlocked more of the secrets about becoming a great leader than any other principle or program he'd ever encountered. I sat rapt, ready to hear the secrets revealed as McBride took me back forty-five years, to April 12, 1957.

April 12, 1957

When I landed the position at General Technologies, I sailed down Austin's Speedway Avenue to the School of Business, ran up three escalators, and flew into Dr. Neumann's office.

"Dr. Neumann, I got the job! Can you believe it? General Technologies hired me!"

"That's great! Congratulations, Ted," he said, putting his hand on my arm. "GT is a great company. I'm proud of you. I knew you could do it. What are you going to be doing for the company?"

"I'm going to be a manager in the finance department!" I declared.

"That's great!" Neumann replied. "All those late-night hours you spent studying finance really paid off. You'll be a wonderful asset to the company and a great representative of our program. I know you'll do well."

"Thanks, I certainly hope so," I said, dropping my head. "I've spent so much energy trying to get my degree and get through interviews that I hadn't given much thought as to whether I'm actually up for the job."

Dr. Neumann silently eyed me from across his desk. "Okay, Ted, what's wrong? Are you afraid you can't do the job? You shouldn't be; with few exceptions, you made straight A's."

"Well, Dr. Neumann, it's not that. It's not the finance part that scares me," I stammered. I was embarrassed to look so weak in front of someone I admired so much.

"Well, what is it, then?"

"It's the management part. I'm going to be supervising nine people. I've never supervised one person before, and now I'm going to be supervising *nine*. Dr. Neumann, I have to be honest with you. I'm scared to death at the prospect. I don't even know where to begin." I fumbled with my hands for a few moments, then finally looked up and blurted out, "Can you help me?"

Almost immediately an awkward silence filled the room. I felt like I had just let down my mentor. Jack Neumann taught in one of the best MBA programs in the country. *I can't believe I just did that,* I thought. *He doesn't have a lot of spare time on his hands, especially for students who already occupy nine-tenths of his every waking hour.*

Dr. Neumann sat in silence, staring a hole through me as if he were weighing an idea. Finally, after what seemed like an eternity, he spoke.

"Ted, I've never known a student, including you, who didn't have spring fever this close to the end of the program. It's difficult enough for students not to mentally check out of here, especially after they land a job. I'm also aware that you have big assignments due in your strategy and finance classes and a final exam in B-Law that comprises 100 percent of your grade. I can teach you the secrets of managing people, but you'll have to keep up your course load *and* give me your Saturdays from here to graduation."

Now it was my turn to stare back at him. He was right. I *did* have spring fever. I counted MBA School as one of the greatest experiences of my life, but all I wanted now was *out*. Neumann interrupted my thoughts.

"Ted, I don't mind giving you my Saturdays, but I won't do it if you don't have a teachable spirit. The opportunity cost of my time is too high. Think it over and call me tonight to let me know what you decide."

That evening I went home and mulled it over. *Surely, GT would train me,* I thought. Then again, Neumann was no mere college professor with his nose stuck in a textbook. He was voted Outstanding Professor of the Year a half-dozen times, partly because he had real-world experience. In fact, he still had a thriving consulting practice.

I didn't have to think long. "I must be insane," I said out loud as I dialed Dr. Neumann's number. But before I could change my mind and hang up, he answered the phone.

"Hello," he said.

"Dr. Neumann . . ."

"Yes, Ted. What did you decide?"

"I've decided to do it."

"Good," he said. "Be at the Business School on the corner of Speedway and Inner Campus Drive at 8:00 A.M. tomorrow. I'll swing by and pick you up. Oh, and wear a pair of jeans you don't mind getting dirty."

I hung up the phone, my mind buzzing with questions. *What had I gotten myself into? Jeans?*

Despite my reservations, at eight the next morning I stood on the corner, wondering if I wasn't the dumbest MBA on campus. I already had my job, after all.

A moment later, an old, beat-up pickup with fading paint pulled around the corner and stopped in front of me. The passenger door flew open and, to my astonishment, there sat Dr. Neumann, dressed in a T-shirt, faded jeans, and a pair of worn-out cowboy boots. I had never seen him wear anything but a coat and tie. Before I knew it, we were squeaking and bouncing our way to Neumann's ranch home in the Texas hill country. Pulling off the farm-to-market road, we wound our way up the long driveway to his ranch. The size and beauty of the ranch struck me. *Maybe I should get into consulting,* I thought.

Halfway to the ranch house, he turned onto a side road. About a half mile down on the right, I saw a large, picturesque pond, bordered on one side by a row of old oak trees. Their giant limbs fanned out, throwing shade over the meadow behind them. There, in the shadow of the trees, lay a small flock of sheep. Dr. Neumann pulled the truck off the side of the road and killed the engine.

"Here we are," he said, turning with a grin. "I need to check out my sheep."

I stared out the window. "Really?"

"Yes. I always check my flock first thing in the morning. I usually check them before now, but I thought you might want to watch."

You've got to be kidding, I thought. "Sounds great," I said. I turned my head so he couldn't see me roll my eyes. I was putting in terribly long study hours. Had I known about this little detour, I would have been more than happy to get an extra few minutes of sleep, while he checked his sheep out on his own. Still, I figured it wouldn't take long. We would get to the management lesson soon enough.

"Who would have thought," I said as I reached for the door handle, "one of the top business school professors and consultants in the country tends sheep!"

Neumann laughed as he got out of the truck. "Don't give my secret away! Besides, I love these sheep. They bring back great memories for me."

"They do?" I asked.

"I grew up in Wyoming, where my dad operated a large sheep ranch," he explained. "I used to work summers, tending sheep as a ranch hand. It was a great learning experience."

Despite my regret over losing precious Saturday morning sleep, a powerful sense of curiosity began to sweep over me. As Neumann walked to the gate, I saw every sheep in the flock get to its feet and amble over to meet him—large, well-fed sheep. When he joined them in the pasture, the sheep started bleating.

"They look excited to see you," I said.

"The feeling's mutual," he replied. "They either see me or my ranch hand at least twice a day. They'll follow me all over this pasture." He reached down to pet one of the sheep. "Come on in. They won't bite, if you're nice."

"Oh-kaaaay," I said as I entered the pen. Some of the sheep momentarily stepped back. Then, as if they felt reassured that I was safe, they surrounded me as they did Neumann.

"Man, these sheep stink," I said out loud.

Neumann laughed. "Ted, that's a tiptoe through the tulips for me. What did you expect, a new-car smell? Help me out here. How many sheep do you count?"

I did a quick canvass and answered, "I think, forty-two. It's difficult to tell with them moving about."

"Good," Neumann said. "That's what I count, and that's how many are supposed to be in here."

"Great," I replied. "Well, I suppose that about wraps it up?"

"Not quite. We're not done yet."

Dr. Neumann began to check out every sheep in his pasture, looking over every one from head to hoof. When he started checking their skin to make sure they had no worms, scabs, or any sign of disease, I was glad I had skipped breakfast.

Next he checked their hooves to make sure they weren't split or infected. "They look pretty good," he said. "It won't get too difficult for them for another month or so."

"Summer heat gets to them?" I asked.

"Well, that and the flies," Neumann replied.

"The flies?" I didn't know if I wanted to hear what was next.

"Yes, they come out during the summer. Deerflies, horseflies, ticks, flees, gnats, and mosquitoes. The worst are the nasal flies."

"Nasal flies?"

"They fly up a sheep's nose and lay eggs in the nasal membranes," Neumann explained. "From there, the flies crawl up the sinuses and into the sheep's head, where they make their home. The irritation drives the sheep crazy. Come summer, we'll have to dip each sheep in bug spray to protect them."

"Glad I asked," I said, certain I was about to lose my lunch before I even ate breakfast. "Are we ready now, Dr. Neumann?"

"Almost. I need to take a quick look at the fence line and the pond. It won't take long."

Over the next fifteen minutes I watched Dr. Neumann check the pond to make sure the water was drinkable and inspect most of the perimeter of his fence line. Along the way, he stopped to use the heel of his boot to fill in a hole that some animal had dug under the fence. He also checked out the pasture to make sure no poisonous plants had sprung up. Finally, he said, "Let's head up to the ranch house. I'll cook us a late breakfast."

Fifty-five minutes later, after a hearty breakfast and two cups of strong coffee, we cleared off the table. Wiping off the still-warm black skillet, Neumann looked at me and asked, "Are you ready?"

"I sure am," I replied. "Let's get down to business."

"Great! Come on and I'll drop you off back at school."

I felt stunned. "What!" I protested. "What do you mean 'back at school'? I thought I gave up my Saturday to learn how to lead people. All we've done is traipse around a bunch of smelly sheep! When are we going to get to the first lesson?"

Neumann calmly eyed his skillet without looking up. "We already have—and they're *not* a bunch of smelly sheep."

"What do you mean, 'We already have'?" I insisted. "Am I missing something here?"

Neumann put down the skillet, walked over to the other side of the table, and sat down. "You've already had your first lesson in managing people," he said evenly, "and, yes, you missed it. But I'm not surprised; many managers do."

The lump of frustration in my throat grew even larger as I seesawed between feeling like I had just wasted my time to feeling like I had just missed what I came to learn. "When did I receive this lesson?" I asked meekly. "Out in the pasture?"

"Exactly."

I gave Dr. Neumann a blank stare.

"Look," he said. "When you start work at General Technologies, you're going to begin with a flock of nine people. To be a successful leader, you're going to have to interact with them in much the same way that a shepherd interacts with his sheep. Ted, your financial skills are great, and you need that to get started, but to really succeed, it's going to take more than that, much more. GT isn't going to promote you into an area where you'll oversee more people until you do well with the nine you already have. So if you want to learn to be a great leader, you're going to have to learn the Way of the Shepherd."

"The Way of the Shepherd?" I asked timidly.

"Yes," Neumann said. "I told you earlier that I grew up working on my dad's sheep ranch. I also told you that I learned a great deal out on the Wyoming grasslands."

"Yes, I remember. Go on."

"What you don't know is that I couldn't wait to leave my dad's ranch and get to where the action was. I wanted to go to the big city and make my way in the world of commerce. You remember the first day of class when I told all of you how I had come out of the corporate world?"

"Yes."

"Well, I had a very successful career there. Like you, I started out at an entry-level managerial post. By the time I left, however, I was executive vice president of the company."

"Okay."

"When I started out, I quickly realized that during all of those years when I thought I was wasting myself on a bunch of sheep, out in the backlands of nowhere, I was in fact learning how to lead people. More importantly, I was learning how to lead them in a way that made them want to follow."

"C'mon, Dr. Neumann," I objected. "Are you *serious?*"

Neumann looked me straight in the eye. "I'm dead serious, Ted. I learned how to shepherd *people*. If you want to be successful, you're going to have to learn how to shepherd people too."

"The Way of the Shepherd?" I repeated.

"Yes. Once you learn the seven principles of the Way of the Shepherd, you will be a very skilled leader indeed."

"So what's the first principle?" I asked.

"You mean the one you just missed?"

"Very funny. What am I supposed to do, check my people for ticks? Please, Dr. Neumann, you're going to have to help me out a little here. You know I'm not exactly used to getting up at the crack of dawn on Saturday."

A sly smile spread over Neumann's face. He rose from the table and walked into the kitchen. Before I had time to protest, he returned with another pot of coffee, filled our cups to the brim, and told me to get out my notebook. He sat down, took a long sip from his coffee, and stared intently at me from across the table. Finally he put his cup down, leaned forward, and in a low voice said, "Ted, the first principle of the Way of the Shepherd is to *always know the condition of your flock!*"

I started taking notes.

"A manager can't manage what he doesn't know," he continued. "So you have to make a point of knowing not just the status of the work but also the status of your people. Many managers focus too much on their projects and not enough on their people. They do what you did when we walked the flock this morning. They're there with their flock—but not really. They're preoccupied with the work and not with the workers."

"Well, the work has to be done," I observed.

"Yes, it does. But remember, it's your *people* who get the job done. Your people are your greatest competitive advantage. Managers will say they agree with that, but often they merely give lip service to the idea."

"I know what you mean," I broke in. "I used to have a boss who talked a good game but never followed through. Whenever anything went wrong, he would pound us into the ground and then turn around and expect us to do our best work for him. Then when things went well, he never paid us a bit of attention. It was a miserable experience."

"Ted," Neumann continued, "that's exactly why the first principle of the Way of the Shepherd is to know the condition of your flock."

"How do I do that?" I asked.

"First, remember that when we checked out the flock this morning, we did it one sheep at a time. The nine people who will report to you at General Technologies may be part of the same flock, but they're individuals, and that's exactly how they'll want to be treated. Believe me, people are tired of being treated like a number. Each person who reports to you will want you to treat him or her not just as an employee but as an individual."

"That sounds good," I said, "but how, specifically, do you do that?"

"You have to take a personal interest in each of the people who report directly to you," Neumann answered. "You need to discover their skills and interests. You need to know their goals and dreams, what motivates them when they walk through the door in the morning, what their career ambitions and frustrations are. In other words, Ted, you have to make a point of knowing what things are impacting them at the moment."

"And how am I supposed to learn *that*?" I asked.

"By engaging your people on a regular basis," Neumann replied. "I told you earlier that either I or my ranch hand circulate among the flock at least twice a day. When you get to General Technologies, you're going to have to do the same thing. You're going to have to get out and get among your people. When you do, keep your eyes and ears open and ask lots of questions. Most importantly, follow through. If an employee requests time to take his child to the doctor, for example, the next time you see him, ask how the child is doing. As best you can, keep up with what's going on in the lives of your people. That sounds easy to do, but it's next to impossible if you don't do the last thing."

"And what's the last thing?" I asked.

"You have to really care about your people. You can go through all the right mechanics, but if you don't genuinely care about the people who report to you, you'll never be the kind of leader they'll drop everything to follow. If they're nothing but stinking sheep to you, they'll never do their best work for you and they won't stay in your fold for long. It's an old adage, but it's true: people don't care how much you know until they know how much you care.

"Anyway," Neumann concluded, "I've given you enough to think about for today. You need to get back to your other schoolwork. Let's head back to campus."

It was a quiet ride back to the university. Dr. Neumann *had* given me a lot to think about. I cracked open my notebook and looked at the notes I had written:

> THE WAY OF THE SHEPHERD
>
> 1. Know the Condition of Your Flock
>   - Follow the status of your people as well as the status of the work.
>   - Get to know your flock, one sheep at a time.
>   - Engage your people on a regular basis.
>   - Keep your eyes and ears open, question, and follow through.

Before I knew it, Dr. Neumann had dropped me off in front of the Business School. As I watched him drive away, I couldn't help but think I was about to get more than I had ever bargained for.

CHAPTER 2

Discover the Shape of Your Sheep

The next Saturday morning I drove up to the Hill Country Livestock Auction and Exchange. I had almost forgotten the events of the previous Saturday as the flood of preparations for exams and papers had pushed their way to the front burner. On the way up, I tried to reconnect with the lessons Dr. Neumann had taught me just a week before.

Always know the condition of your flock, I thought as I tried to shake the sleep out of my head. *Get to know your flock one sheep at a time. Engage your people and follow through.*

Dr. Neumann was waiting for me as I pulled into the livestock exchange. I parked my DeSoto among the rows of pickup trucks and hopped out just as he reached my car. "Don't you have any boots?" he asked, looking at my new penny loafers.

"What's wrong with penny loafers?" I asked indignantly.

"Uh, not a thing," he said. "But this ought to be entertaining, at least."

About that time I managed to take a deep breath and smelled one of the foulest odors I'd ever inhaled. A pungent amalgamation of rotting hay, manure, and animal stench rivaled the reeking fumes emanating from a portapotty at a tractor pull. *Don't mention anything about the sheep stinking,* I thought, remembering he seemed a little touchy on the subject. I guess my nostril flare ultimately gave me away.

"Well," Neumann winked, "I see you're enjoying the fresh country air!"

"Ugh," I said. "Give me smog."

Neumann laughed out loud. "You'll survive. Now come on. There's something I want you to see."

I tried to keep up with him as we headed briskly to the auction ring but quickly fell several steps behind. The livestock grounds were a veritable minefield of droppings that came in all sizes, shapes, and colors. Hopping between the piles and trying in vain to keep up, I couldn't help but think of my dumb question: "What's wrong with penny loafers?"

We entered the auction house to find several rows of tiered aluminum bleacher seats ringing an animal pen. Across from the bleachers sat a large, raised bench for the auctioneers and their assistants. The room filled with ranchers in Stetsons, eager to bid on a ewe in the middle of the pen. Three auction-house assistants stood down below, directly in front of the ring of bidders, scanning the audience for any signs of a bid. The endless drone of the auctioneer intermittently stopped as a rancher raised his hand to bid. An assistant would point one hand straight in the air and the other hand at the bidder and yell out, "Hep!"

We stood at the back and watched the ballet of bidding as one animal after another entered the pen for auction. Neumann leaned over and whispered, "This is where it starts. This is where building and leading a great team begins. These sheep ranchers are building their flocks here."

For a moment our attention flew back to the room as we heard the assistants yell a flurry of, "Hep," "Hep," "Hep."

"Okay," I said, "it doesn't look too difficult to me. They see a sheep they like, hold up their hand, and bid. What's so difficult about that?"

At that moment the auctioneer slammed a knob of wood to his desk and yelled, "Sold!"

Neumann leaned closer. "*Now* take a look." After the auctioneer had registered the sale of the animal, almost every rancher there pulled a piece of paper out of his pocket, scribbled a few lines on it, and put it back in his pocket. Neumann continued, "The bidding is the easy part. Each shepherd has done his homework before coming to the auction ring. They're checking the prices of each animal and waiting until the lot they're interested in comes up for auction. The point is they know what they're after."

"And what's that?" I asked.

"Come on and I'll show you. Let's look at the holding pens."

Once again, Neumann took off like a shot and I followed as closely as I could, trying to keep my penny loafers as clean as possible.

Standing next to one of the sheep pens, Neumann looked at me and said, "Okay, you're one of the ranchers up in the auction house. Which one of these animals would you bid for?"

"Well, that one looks pretty good, I suppose." In fact, I couldn't really tell much of a difference between one sheep and another.

"That would be a poor choice," he declared.

"How so?" I asked. "They all look pretty much the same to me. What makes one better than the other?"

"Take a closer look," Neumann said. "Look carefully." He bent down and pointed out problems in the sheep I had selected. "You want a straight topline, not a rough one like this sheep has. You also want firm, straight legs with trim shoulders and a good width across the rib cage and chest."

"Why is that important?" I wondered aloud.

"Because you're looking for healthy, productive sheep. It's like this, Ted. As a shepherd, your choice of sheep can make flock management easier or harder.[1] If you don't buy right, you'll inherit someone else's problems."

I thought a moment and said, "I suppose it's like the draft in football. Each team is very particular about the players they choose because they know that whoever fields the best team usually wins."

"That's a pretty good analogy," Neumann said.

"Thanks," I replied. "So what am I supposed to look for at General Technologies to make sure I have a healthy, productive flock?"

"Good question; that shows you're thinking," Neumann said. "Back when I was a manager, I always tried to make sure that anyone I interviewed was a good fit both for the company and for the position. I also wanted to make sure that my existing employees fit their positions well too."

"So how did you do that?" I asked.

Neumann smiled. "Well, just as each sheep has its own particular shape or makeup, so does each person in the company. So I examine their shape to make sure they're a good fit."

I thought for a moment to see if I could guess the catch. "Okay," I finally said. "I'll take the hook. What do you mean, you 'examine their shape to make sure they're a good fit'? Can't you get in trouble doing that?"

Neumann pulled himself up onto the top rail of the fence, pulled a piece of paper out of his pocket, and motioned for me to join him. Then he wrote the word SHAPE down the left side of the paper.[2] "Here are the things I look for to make sure I'm not trying to fit a square peg into a round hole," he said.

S—Strengths

"First, I want to make sure each person has the skill set needed to do the job. Sometimes they can learn it on the job. Sometimes they have to have it on the day they arrive. It depends on the position. The point is I always try to place people where they can operate out of their strengths and not their weaknesses. So the first step is to understand the strengths of the people on your team, or the people who are about to join it."

H—Heart

"While your strengths reflect your abilities, your heart reflects your passion," Neumann explained. "There's nothing more commonplace than a company full of bright, talented people who are completely unmotivated to do their work. It doesn't matter how strong you are in a given area if you're not motivated to exercise that strength, so I want to know what my people are passionate about. If I put them in areas that reflect their passions, they'll arrive to work like they've been shot out of a cannon. They'll begin to think of their job more as a cause than as a place to draw a paycheck. That's a big difference!"

A—Attitude

"I can't emphasize this one enough," Neumann said. "You want positive, can-do people. Given a choice between talent and attitude, I'll take attitude every time."

"Why is that?" I asked.

"For one thing, people with a good attitude are usually team players. For another, they usually have a teachable spirit. People with negative attitudes tend to be lone rangers. You can't teach them a thing."

"I can understand choosing attitude over talent in an ideal world," I replied, "but what if the person with the bad attitude also happens to be your best performer? What do you do then?"

Neumann paused. "Ted, you get rid of them."

"But if you get rid of your star performer," I said, "then the performance of your team falls. Wouldn't it be better to help the person develop a positive attitude instead?"

"No, because people with negative attitudes don't have a learner's heart. Dumping such individuals off your team will hurt in the short run, but not in the long run. You have to remember that star performers with an attitude put a constant drag on everyone else. The price you pay for their performance is constant agitation. People with negative attitudes can't help but stir the pot."

Neumann took a deep breath, then continued. "There's one other big reason to show them the door. They're poor examples for the rest of your people. If you compromise with negative people for the sake of their abilities, your other people will learn their bad habits. I've seen one person's bad attitude spread like a cancer through an entire office."

"That's true," I agreed. "When I was an undergrad, I did a summer internship at a bank. I was thrilled to be there. There was one man, though, who criticized everything. He kept spouting off about the mistakes management was making. It wasn't long before I couldn't wait until quitting time. After a while I thought maybe I had made a mistake in going there."

"That's it exactly," Neumann said. "Such people propagate the greener-grass syndrome. You remember the hole under the fence that I had to fill in when we walked the pasture, back at the ranch?"

"Sure," I said.

"Well, the ewe that dug it was the best sheep I had.[3] She had the prettiest wool of any in the flock and was as strong as an ox. The only problem was she had a bad attitude."

"I didn't know a sheep could have an attitude!" I said, laughing.

"You better believe it. She was always butting heads with the younger ewes to let them know who was the boss. What's more, she was a fence crawler. She was always probing for a way to get into the neighbor's pasture. I have some of the lushest pasture in the Texas hill country, but she always thought the grass was greener on the other side of my fence. I knew I was going to have to take action when my younger lambs started to mimic her by digging under the fence. I wish she would have enjoyed everything I had prepared for her, but she just wasn't content with what she had."

Neumann paused, then said, "Now that I think about it, she reminds me of a young colleague of mine years ago at the university. This ambitious young professor made a point of telling the dean that he had a great opportunity at another university. The young buck didn't really want to leave but thought he could use the situation to get a raise out of the old dean."

"So what did the dean do?" I asked.

"He adjusted his spectacles, turned up his hearing aid, got up from his leather chair, waddled around the corner of his desk, stuck out his hand to the young prof, and said, 'I want to be the first to wish you well in your new endeavor. The last thing I would ever want would be to hold back the career of someone as bright as you.' Then the dean said that since finals had ended, he knew the professor wouldn't mind cleaning out his office quickly, as we would have to start work right away on finding his replacement."

Neumann chuckled. "I haven't thought about that story in years," he said. "That young man entered the dean's office like he was going to put one over on the old man, and he left like a whipped puppy."

"That sure taught him a lesson," I said.

"And the rest of the faculty," Neumann replied. "The dean wasn't about to let the greener-grass syndrome take over because of one discontented, ambitious person."

"Speaking of greener grass," I said, "what did you do with the ewe that caused you so many problems?"

"I got two words for you, Ted: lamb chops! Now let's cover the other two items and head back to the ranch. There's work to be done, and I don't want us to waste any time."

P—Personality

"Each one of us has been hardwired with a distinct personality," Neumann continued. "Some of us are wired to be extroverts; others, introverts. Some people love repetition. They love knowing that they're going to do the same thing in their job tomorrow that they did today. Others would sooner crawl down into a hole and die if they can't have some variety. Some people thrive on structure. Some thrive on change. The point is to put a person in a position that reflects his or her personality. Let me give you a heads-up: General Technologies changes *everything* every six months. I would be very careful about hiring anyone who has a low tolerance for change."

E—Experiences

"Ted, notice that I didn't just say *experience*. I said *experiences*. This last point is the most vague, but it's important to mention.

Each person you meet is a product of their life experiences. Often the key to understanding an individual and the key to knowing where to place him or her on your team is to learn something about the person's various experiences. I can't give you a hard rule here, but I can give you an example."

"That would be great," I said.

"I hadn't been at my company too terribly long," he continued, "when I had to hire a project manager to work with a group of our clients. I'd had enough experience with these clients to know they were very demanding and particular. Each one thought their project was the only one we had to do. And they all wanted their projects finished by yesterday. It made for a very precarious situation, and I knew I was going to have to be very careful in picking the right person for the job."

"So what did you do?" I asked.

"I hired a retired minister," Neumann replied.

"You hired a *minister?*"

"I sure did. And most of my peers responded the same way you just did. They all said, 'He doesn't have any *experience*. He doesn't understand the corporate world. All he knows how to do is to preach on Sunday.' It raised quite a ruckus," Neumann continued. "But I knew better. I knew he had the skills for the job, the passion, and the right attitude. But I knew something even more important."

"What's that?" I asked.

"I knew that he was experienced in working with people. I knew that if anyone could work with the egos that the position called for, he could."

"And did he?"

"Let's just say he was a square peg in a square hole!"

On the way to my car, Neumann put his arm around me and gave me some fatherly advice. In that moment, I knew we were moving from a teacher-student relationship to that of a mentor and his protégé. I realize now, of course, that he was starting to shepherd *me*.

"Ted, a couple of other things," Neumann said.

"Okay," I said, "what are they?"

"Don't make the mistake of thinking that what I'm teaching you is just for you to use with other people. It's for you, too."

"What do you mean?" I wondered aloud.

Neumann looked down thoughtfully and then at me. Without breaking stride, he said, "Ted, most people spend years struggling to find their calling in life. I was one of them. I spent years doing other things that I was pretty good at, but I always felt something was missing. Until I discovered teaching, I felt like a square peg in a round hole. Once I found the classroom, I knew I had found my life purpose. Teaching reflects who I am. More than anything else, it reflects my strengths, passions, attitudes, and personality traits. Teaching business also takes advantage of the experiences I've had in the corporate world. Ted, if you want to find your calling in life, if, at the very least, you want to make sure you're working in an area where you have the greatest potential for success, then take a look at *your* SHAPE and make sure that you're a good fit for your job."

We stopped at the door of my car, and Neumann announced, "There's your homework for tonight. I want you to write out a profile of your SHAPE." Then he patted me on my shoulder and grinned.

"Dr. Neumann, you said there were a couple of things," I reminded him. "What's the other?"

"Well, if I were you, I'd wipe my shoes off before I got in the car."

I looked down and almost screamed. "My shoes! My brand new penny loafers! I'll never get them clean! They're covered in cow manure and dirt." I turned in exasperation to Neumann. "I don't have any paper towels in my car. What am I supposed to do?"

"I don't have the *foggiest* idea," he said. "You could take a course on crisis management. At any rate, you're a good student, Ted. I'm sure you can handle it."

After desecrating the school newspaper with my shoes, I sat in my DeSoto thinking while Neumann went inside to finalize his purchase. At that point I wasn't sure I could handle much of anything. I found myself starting to warm to the idea of managing *people*, however, after jotting down some notes on my second session with Dr. Neumann:

The Way of the Shepherd

2. Discover the Shape of Your Sheep
   - Your choice of sheep can make flock management easier or harder.
   - Start with healthy sheep, or you'll inherit someone else's problems.
   - Know the SHAPE of your sheep to make sure they're in the right fold.

CHAPTER 3

Help Your Sheep Identify with You

The drive from the auction house to the ranch gave me a few minutes alone to ponder what Dr. Neumann had said. I had been so busy trying to get through school that I hadn't given much thought as to what career would be the best fit for me. I just knew that I wanted to work for a big company like General Technologies.

Then I thought about the nine people who would report to me. I began to see how the success of our small department would depend on making sure those people were in the right place. I wondered if their strengths and passions would reflect their responsibilities. "I want my people to have a heart for what they do," I said aloud, my thoughts punctuating the air. "I want them to feel excited about coming in to work in the morning." It began to dawn on me that the effectiveness of my little flock, as well as the fulfillment of each person in it, depended on what kind of a shepherd-leader I would be.

No sooner had I parked my car in the barn driveway than Neumann pulled up beside me in his old, beat-up Ford. Standing in the truck bed was the largest ewe I had ever seen. (Not that I had seen that many.) "C'mon and give me a hand," he said through the open window. "Unload her and put her in the pen over there while I get some tools out of the barn. I'll meet you there in a minute. It's almost time for your next lesson."

Several minutes later, the new ewe and I were staring at one another within the confines of the holding pen. She looked more unruffled than I did. I'm not sure, but I think she had ended up carrying *me* into the pen. When I looked up, I saw Neumann standing at the fence post, wearing the grin to which I had become all too accustomed. "Time for your next lesson," he said.

"Thanks for the warning," I responded, dusting the wool and dirt off my pants. "I can hardly wait."

Neumann walked over and put his hand on my shoulder. "Time to put your mark on her."

"Um . . . what do you mean?" I asked.

"It means it's time for you to tag her," Neumann replied, staring right at me.[1]

"And how am I supposed to do *that*?" I inquired.

"With these," he said, opening his hand. There on his palm lay a pair of stainless steel pliers with deep jaws, long handles, and a needlelike piercing tooth. Beside the pliers lay a bright yellow tag with a number and Neumann's ranch symbol on it. I remembered seeing similar tags on the ears of the sheep when we had walked Neumann's pasture the week before.

"This goes on her ear?" I asked, hoping to hear something different.

"Yep," Neumann said, dropping the tag and pliers into my hand.

"But won't that hurt? I mean that has to be *painful*, doesn't it?"

"Yes," Neumann replied. "It's very painful. Ear tissue is sensitive."

"But why?" I asked, handing the pliers back to Neumann. "What's the point?"

"The point is," Neumann said carefully, "that the tag identifies the ewe as belonging to this flock. And if you're a good shepherd and care about your sheep, you'll put the tag on her." He opened his hand, inviting me to take back the pliers. We stared at each other, and after a moment or two, I relented. I retrieved the pliers, and after Neumann showed me what to do, I walked into the pen, where moments before I had felt nothing but anger for this stupid sheep. Now I felt nothing but pity and guilt. (Then I remembered my first encounter with the hearty ewe and secretly wondered if I wouldn't be coming out of the pen with the tag in *my* ear.)

Feeling the cold weight of the stainless steel in my hand reminded me of the pain I was about to inflict on this helpless animal. I had to hold her up close and tight as I brought the pliers to her ear. With a strong squeeze of the handle, I drove the pin and the tag through her skin. The stunned sheep tried to lurch away in pain. I released her and the handle as quickly as I could so that I wouldn't tear the sensitive tissues in her ear. I felt horrible.

"C'mon," Neumann said, "let's head up to the house and have a talk over a Coca-Cola." Minutes later, we were sitting in his den, cooling off. "I feel terrible," I said, breaking the silence.

"It hurt you too, didn't it?"

"Yeah," I replied. "I didn't want to do it."

"Better get used to it. It comes with the territory," Neumann declared. "When you're in a position of leadership, there are going to come times when you have to inflict pain on the people you oversee. There'll be reprimands, poor performance reviews, and times when you have to let people go. You won't want to do those things either, but you will if you're a good shepherd."

Nodding to show that I understood, I said, "One question, though. I noticed that when I punctured her ear with the pliers, she lurched away from me but didn't cry out. How come?"

"Well," Neumann replied, "sometimes sheep are the most stupid creatures on earth. I've seen a forty-pound lamb repeatedly try to jump through a six-inch square hole in the fence. So you know they're not the sharpest knives in the drawer. At other times, however, they're pretty shrewd. They know the only defense they have against a coyote—which still isn't much—is to stay with the flock. That's why their flocking instincts are so strong. They know that coyotes will prey on the weakest animal they can single out from the flock. So sheep rarely cry out when they're in pain because they know it will draw the attention of their predators."

Neumann then shifted his gaze to me. "Now let's talk about the flock you're going to shepherd at General Technologies," he said. "How do you turn a collection of individual sheep, bordered by the same fence, into a flock?"

"Well," I replied, "I know from our talk at the auction house that it starts with making the right choices about who is going to be a part of my team and making sure they are placed in an area that reflects their SHAPE."

"Good. You've been listening," Neumann said. "That allows each member of your team to work in an area where they know they can make a difference. In short, not only will they be effective in their work, but they will also enjoy a measure of fulfillment in it. That's not the whole story, however. Not only do you want to leverage the performance of each person in your outfit, you also want to leverage the performance of the group as a whole."

"And that's done by . . . ?"

"By doing what you did a little while ago," Neumann said.

"Tagging their ears?" I said, smiling.

"By putting your mark on your sheep," Neumann replied. "I told you earlier that the tag identifies the sheep as belonging to the flock. In many ways, Ted, people are a lot like sheep. Like sheep, people have a powerful flocking instinct. They have a tremendous need to belong. Great leaders understand that instinct and tap into it."

"How do they do that?" I asked.

"Great leaders instill a sense of meaning and belonging in their followers by putting the personal imprint of who they are and what they stand for on their people. That imprint becomes the common ground where the people collectively meet and identify with their leader. A leader's personal mark, in other words, becomes the common denominator of the organization."

Neumann gestured toward the sheep and said, "The tag you put on that ewe out there stands for something, Ted. It stands for me as its shepherd. Even though our flock is small, this ranch has a reputation for producing outstanding livestock. That tag you put on the ewe is a mark of excellence. It's just the same as writing my name across the side of that sheep. Your employees at General Technologies will bear your mark, just as that sheep bears mine. They will bear a mark that will tell people what kind of a shepherd-leader you really are. Make sure that your mark of leadership stands for something great, Ted, and you will have a great following! Now, come on and let's check on our ewe, shall we?"

As we walked silently down the ranch house road, I digested what Dr. Neumann had just told me. I knew he had presented a profound truth about the tremendous need people have to belong and about the importance of the mark that a leader imprints on those who follow him. I wanted to know more. So I finally asked him, "Dr. Neumann, what is the mark of a great leader?"

He took a deep breath and said, "I can tell you one of the marks of a *good* leader. He doesn't do the thinking for his people. Now you tell me what the mark of a *great* leader is."

By this time my brain was on overload. This was definitely *not* the response I wanted from Dr. Neumann. A dozen quality traits buzzed through my mind. Finally, grasping for straws,

I said the first thing that popped into my mind: "The greatest leader I know is my dad. But of course he's not an example of a great business leader, is he? He's a school teacher." I said it quietly, almost like an apology.

"That's fine," said Dr. Neumann. "Leadership takes place in the home and schoolroom as well as in the boardroom. What is it that makes your dad such a great leader?"

Then it hit me. How could I have missed it? "My father is a man of unquestioned integrity," I replied. "It doesn't matter what the issue is, my father is going to be on the side of what's right, no matter how much it costs him."

"Go on," Dr. Neumann said.

"Dad taught us not to compromise. He always says, 'A man can sell his integrity for a nickel, but all the money in the world won't buy it back again.'"

"That's great, Ted," Neumann replied. "What else stands out about your father?"

It was back to the mental think tank. After a few moments I answered, "Probably two or three things."

"Okay, what's the first one?" Dr. Neumann asked.

"First, my dad is the same man in private as he is in public. It doesn't matter whether he's at church, before the school board, or at home. What you see is what you get."

An old memory surfaced, and I said, "I remember going on a fishing trip with my best friend and his dad. His dad was chairman of the deacons at our church. I was always impressed with him when he stood to speak to the congregation. Out on the lake, however, he became a totally different person. He told jokes and made off-color remarks that I know he would never say in church. I lost a lot of respect for him that day. I knew my dad would never do that."

"What you're saying," Dr. Neumann commented, "is that your dad is authentic."

"Absolutely," I replied. "Dad is the real McCoy."

"This is great," Neumann said. "What's the second thing?"

"Well, my dad sets pretty high standards. He expects my sister and me to do our very best. Dad says it's good to stretch ourselves every now and then so that we're always growing. He says if we don't, we won't know what we're capable of."

"I couldn't have put it better myself," Dr. Neumann said. "What else?"

"Well, I think what I like best about him is that he deals compassionately with us when we screw up. One Sunday afternoon after I got my driver's license, I took his car without permission and nearly demolished it. When I got home, Dad was waiting for me. I thought the sky would fall. The first thing he did, however, was grab me and hug me close. I was totally shocked. He had tears in his eyes. Then, of course, about the time I thought I was going to live, I thought he was going to kill me. I never forgot that he hugged me first, though. I had to work the entire summer to pay the car-repair bill, but I always knew it wasn't the car that he cared about. It was me."

Dr. Neumann looked at me for a long moment and said, "Ted, let me ask you a question. Do you *trust* your dad?"

"With my life," I immediately replied. "Why do you ask?"

"Because everything you've told me about your dad tells me he's a man who can be trusted."

"Yes," I said. "A lot of people besides me trust my dad."

"That," Dr. Neumann said, "is the mark of a great leader. When you get to General Technologies, the nine people in your department are all going to ask themselves two questions. First, Does he know what he's doing? And second, Can I trust him? Ted, I have no doubt that where you're concerned, the answer to both questions will be yes. But even if they answer the first question with a no, they'll forgive you if they can answer the second question with a yes."

I nodded and Neumann continued. "People long to follow a leader who is a person of integrity, authenticity, and compassion. That person will have the loyal following and trust of his people. I'm glad you have a father like that, Ted. I know you'll be able to leave a mark of excellence on your people at GT, because it's been modeled for you at home."

About that time, we arrived at the holding pen. Neumann stopped at the gate, looked at me and said, "Ted, there's at least one more part of the answer to your question."

"And what is that?" I asked.

"Great leaders leave their mark by constantly communicating their values and sense of mission. They tirelessly call their people to engage in the cause. They know people are easily distracted by the many pulls of life, so they're continually calling them back to the mission, back to their purpose for being.

"Pick any great leader you can think of. General Patton incessantly demanded that his troops stay on the move. Jesus relentlessly appealed to his followers to spread the good news of the kingdom. Lincoln constantly declared that the Union must be preserved. See?

"Ted, when you get to GT, define the cause for your nine people and help them to see where they fit in it. Let them know that without your department and without each member's special part, General Technologies could not provide the goods and services that have improved the lives of millions of people. And don't forget to ask for their commitment to the cause.

"Okay," Neumann said, "end of sermon. Let's check our ewe!"

My mentor watched from the distance as I walked into the pen with outstretched arms and open hands. I wanted the ewe to see that I held no pliers this time around. To my astonishment, she allowed me to walk right up to her. I had never talked to a sheep before. But I did that day.

I told her how sorry I was to cause her any pain. I told her how important it was for her to wear the mark of her shepherd and what a great flock she was a part of. All the while I talked, I ran my hands through her thick, silky wool. She felt soft to the touch, and this time she was gentle. Part of me couldn't believe I was really talking to a *sheep*.

From the fence line I heard Neumann's voice call out, "Ted, so far you haven't disappointed me!"

"What do you mean?" I asked.

"Well," he said, "the last point of your lesson today is this: you can't make your mark on the people you lead unless you get up close and personal. You've ended this afternoon the way you started it, by holding your sheep up close to you, first to cause pain and now to offer encouragement. Every day at General Technologies, you're going to make a decision about the way you lead. You can do it from afar, or you can do it up close and personal. You can impress from afar, but to influence, to really leave your mark, you're going to have to do it personally. Remember, Ted, for great leaders, leadership isn't just professional; it's personal. I'll see you next week in class."

That evening, back at my apartment, I wrote down everything I had learned that day. The new material in my notebook looked like this:

THE WAY OF THE SHEPHERD

3. Help Your Sheep Identify with You
   - Build trust with your followers by modeling authenticity, integrity, and compassion.
   - Set high standards of performance.
   - Relentlessly communicate your values and sense of mission.
   - Define the cause for your people and tell them where they fit in.
   - Remember that great leadership isn't just professional; it's personal.

CHAPTER 4

Make Your Pasture A Safe Place

The following week took a lot out of me. We had a slew of papers due that week, and with the end of the semester and graduation quickly approaching, the competition was growing fierce. All of us were judged against each other, which made for an interesting mix of competition and cooperation ("coopetition," according to business school).[1]

Late Thursday night Dr. Neumann called me at home.

"Ted, Jack Neumann. How are you holding up?"

"Okay, I suppose, considering I've averaged about four hours of sleep a night this week."

"Well, hang in there," Neumann counseled me. "You don't have much further to go. You'll get there before you know it. In fact, that's why I'm calling."

"Okay," I said.

"I was calling to see if we could meet tomorrow after my class instead of Saturday morning," he explained.

"That's fine with me," I replied. "But why the change?"

"I figure you could use a Saturday off."

"Thanks," I said. "I'm certainly not going to argue with you. I wouldn't mind having a day to sleep in."

"Good," Neumann answered. "Meet me out in front of the Business School after class and I'll pick you up. See you tomorrow."

After Dr. Neumann's lecture on conglomerates, I went outside to scan the street for my mentor's red pickup. Suddenly a brand-new 1957 red and white Corvette convertible wheeled around the corner and tooted its horn at me. I was surprised to see Dr. Neumann sitting behind the wheel.

"Hop in!" he said brightly.

"Nice car," I said. "What happened to the pickup?"

"Ted, I didn't get my Ph.D. at Harvard to spend all my time driving around in a beat-up, old pickup truck," he said, grinning broadly.

For the next forty minutes we sped up and down winding country roads, putting the Corvette's suspension through its paces. Finally, Dr. Neumann pulled the car off to the side of the road on a farm-to-market road outside of Austin.

"C'mon," he said. "Time for your next object lesson. I'm pretty certain you'll remember this one."

We hopped out of the car and walked a few steps across a gully to a fence line that paralleled the road.

"Take a look," Neumann said.

Immediately my mouth gaped open. Before me lay one of the most pitiful sights I had ever seen.[2] *Dr. Neumann was right,* I thought. *I will remember this.* "Dr. Neumann, this is horrible."

"Yes, it is, Ted. Now take a close look. Tell me what you see."

"I see poor, emaciated sheep," I said, "with matted, gnarled wool. I see brown grass that looks as if it has been eaten down to the nub." I scanned the horizon and added, "This is awful! I see poor, rundown shelters."

"What else do you see, Ted? Take a closer look."

Leaning forward and straining at the sheep, I could see flies swarming around the heads and eyes of the whole flock. And what I saw next repulsed me. "Oh, this makes me sick," I blurted out. On the backs of the sheep I could see terrible sores infested with bugs.

"Those are blowflies," Neumann explained. "They lay eggs in untended cuts and sores on the sheep. The eggs hatch into maggots and tunnel deep into the sheep's skin. If left untreated, the condition can kill the sheep."

"Who could *do* this to such docile creatures?" I wondered aloud.

"What you see here, Ted," he replied, "is neglect. What you saw back at my place was vigilant care. I wanted you to see the difference. Not all flocks look as good as mine."

"Or pastures," I replied.

"That's a large part of the reason why these sheep are in such pitiful condition," Neumann continued. "The shepherd, if you can call him that, didn't make the pasture a safe place for his flock. He didn't make it a place where his sheep could flourish."

"That's very sad," I answered.

"I'll tell you what else is sad," Neumann added. "Every day, hundreds of thousands of people get up and go to work in a fold that looks a lot like this one. They work in a neglected pasture, untended by the very people who are responsible for the health and well-being of the flock. At quitting time, they go home having survived another day, but they haven't thrived. They certainly haven't flourished. On the outside, Ted, they look just fine, but on the inside, they look like these poor sheep."

"So what does it take, besides the obvious, to give people a safe pasture in which they can flourish?" I asked.

"Great question," Neumann replied. "Let's head back to campus so you can pick up your car, and I'll tell you on the way."

Moments later as we zipped down country roads, Dr. Neumann unfolded his lesson.

"Ted," he began, "a flock can't be productive—it can't produce the best wool and gain the most weight—unless the sheep get the rest and nourishment they need. One of the big reasons those sheep back there look so emaciated is because they are completely exhausted."

He looked briefly in my direction and then continued. "It's a fact that sheep will not lie down and rest unless they feel safe from at least three aggravations.[3] Address the three items and you create a safe pasture where your flock can flourish."

Neumann again took his eye off the road momentarily to look at me while he made his first point. "The first aggravation is fear. The flock must be free from fear," he said.

"The fear of being harmed?" I asked nervously.

"Yes, Ted, the sheep must be free from the fear of being harmed."

"No, Dr. Neumann, I wasn't thinking of the sheep," I said, frantically pointing to the big farm implement immediately in front of us. "More like sheep dip!"

"Very funny," Neumann said, swerving the 'Vette expertly around the pudgy tractor. "Man, I love this car. I couldn't have done that in my old Ford."

"I'll send Chevrolet a thank-you note when I get home," I said, bracing myself in the seat. "In the meantime, you're doing wonders for my prayer life."

"Well, good for you," Neumann said. "I'm sure that won't hurt you one bit. Now back to my sheep."

"Please."

"Where was I?" he asked, one arm flailing in the air. (I started to notice how animated he became the more he talked about his sheep.) "Ah, yes. In order for the pasture to be a safe place, the sheep have to feel secure from predators. If they don't, they constantly stay on their feet, always looking out in case they have to make a run for it. Did you see the fences back there?"

"Yes," I said. "They were in as bad a shape as the shelters. There were sections where the fence had almost come down."

"Sheep may not be the brightest animals on four feet," he declared, "but they know when they're vulnerable. That's why they were all standing. In a more subtle way, we're just like them. Whenever we get a whiff that something's amiss, we instinctively walk around on our tiptoes. It's the uncertainty that gets us."

After thinking about this for a moment, I said, "Dr. Neumann, do you remember the bank, where I did my summer internship?"

"Yes," he replied.

"I worked at that bank for two years after I received my undergrad degree. About the middle of the second year, the bank experienced some financial difficulties. Every two weeks, a rumor went around that we were all about to be laid off. It was terrible. Everyone walked around on eggshells. I kept trying to do my very best work for the company so that if the rumors proved true, I wouldn't get axed. Trouble was, the whole time I was working, I kept wondering if it was all for nothing. It was next to impossible for me to keep my mind on my work."

Dr. Neumann nodded and said, "My point exactly. If you don't feel secure at work, there's no way you can do your best work. Ted, don't forget that! If you couldn't stay focused under those conditions, neither will your people at General Technologies. To do their best work, your people have to feel free from fear."

"How do I manage that?" I asked.

"By doing everything you can to eliminate the uncertainty that's distracting them. You do that by keeping your people well informed. If there's bad news, let your people hear it from you first. If they feel confident that you'll let them know as soon as you know, they'll be less susceptible to the rumor mill. In fact, this is where the flocking instincts of people are bad. If your employees don't trust you to keep them up to date on matters that affect them, all it takes is for one person to hear a piece of bad news, and the next thing you know, your whole department will be standing around the coffeepot."

Neumann again turned to look at me to emphasize his point. "If that happens on a regular basis," he warned, "it's a sign you haven't been a good shepherd to your flock."

"That's a good word," I said, staring nervously at the road in front me.

"One more thing before we move on," Neumann said. "Keep your sheep individually informed, as well as the flock as a whole."

"Regarding what?" I inquired.

"Specifically, regarding their performance. One huge uncertainty that keeps people agitated are year-end reviews. You'll go a long way toward making your pasture a safe place if you keep your people informed on their progress *before* review time. That way they won't be surprised if they receive a negative review, and more importantly, they'll have an opportunity to improve their performance by the time the formal review rolls around."

"Okay," I said. "What's the second agitation that keeps the sheep from flourishing?"

"Rivalry," Neumann said. He paused, then added, "You could do a doctoral dissertation on the drag on earnings brought about by inter- and intra-departmental friction. Rivalry gets people working against one another rather than with one another. There's no telling how many companies have been brought down because the people fought each other rather than the competition."

"And how do you handle that?" I asked.

"You deal with it at its three main sources," Neumann said. "Often tensions rise because people are jockeying for position.

Sheep are usually docile animals, but don't let that fool you; there's a butting order within the flock. Here's another example of how people are just like sheep. We're consumed with where we are in the pecking order."

"Yes," I smiled. "Just like we are in class."

"Absolutely, Ted. That's why the first question students ask when I hand out test scores—"

"Is what was the average." I interrupted.

"See? Everyone wants to know whether their performance was above the average of the class or below. It's human nature to jockey for position."

"So what do I do to address that?"

"You infuse every position with importance," Neumann said, pushing the accelerator a little closer to the floor. "People will be less apt to vie for position if they feel as though their current position has a degree of significance. You let your people at GT know from day one, Ted, that *everyone* is important on your team. Teach your people that each person has a vital role to play. Make them feel like you couldn't do it without them."

In those moments I made a second observation: the faster Neumann talked, the faster the car moved.

"Next," he said, "you cull chronic instigators from the flock. There are some people in life, Ted, who just aren't happy unless they are *un*happy. It takes only one contentious person to destroy the collaborative atmosphere of an entire department. People can't fully focus their attention on a project if they have to constantly keep one eye on another stiff-necked, stubborn sheep." His face grew a faint red. "They make me so mad," he said, and he pushed the accelerator a little further to the floor.

"That goes back to what you said at the auction house about making sure you retain people who have good attitudes," I said as I braced myself in the seat.

"Absolutely," Neumann replied. "By the way, Ted, did you notice the scars and cuts on the sheep back there?"

"Yes," I said, now gripping the armrest with both hands. "They looked horribly infected."

"Yes, but have you figured out why they were cut up in the first place?"

"No," I said. "Were they butting heads to determine the pecking order?"

"No, not this time," he said, shaking his head. "It's pretty sad, really. They were fighting over the same small patch of grass. You'll often find rivalry at its highest, Ted, where you find a lot of people fighting over a little. Smart shepherds protect their flocks from this through pasture rotation. They rotate their flock to fresh, greener fields. That's what the negligent shepherd should have done back there. I don't want to belabor this. Point is: rotate opportunities among the different members of your flock, Ted. That way they won't feel a need to fight for them."

Neumann paused for a second and then added, "You know, as a father of young children, I've learned that it's a smart parent who rotates the chores among the offspring. What could be more discouraging than finding out that you are the designated garbage-child for life?"

He chuckled, then continued. "Okay, the next one isn't as weighty as the first, but it can still affect the productivity of your flock. Aggravation number three: pests."

"Pests? Are you serious?" I asked.

"Absolutely. A pasture that doesn't keep the sheep free from pests is not one where they can flourish. The presence of large numbers of flies and gnats is a constant source of irritation for the sheep. They won't lie down unless they are free from pests. Now, the things that pester people in the workplace obviously aren't of the same sort that animals deal with, but they're no less irritating. Sometimes managers are very adept at creating a whole multitude of annoyances that distract their people from their work."

"Like . . . ?"

"Like, if the dean calls one more meeting for us to discuss our New Orleans MBA extension program, I'll go nuts," Neumann said, gunning the car around the corner and hurtling a little off the road.

"Oh, I get it," I said, wedging myself even tighter in the seat and praying that Dr. Neumann would slow down. "When the bank I worked at was going through its financial difficulty, we went through this huge cost-cutting initiative. Every day I received a ream of memos announcing new cost-cutting measures. I couldn't keep up. One memo they circulated outlawed 'courtesy flushes' in the bathroom."

"No kidding? That would definitely be annoying," Neumann said. "The thing about pests is that they are small. They're miniscule in the larger scheme of things, but they can drive a person to distraction. Things like a constant rearranging of priorities, 'flavor of the month' change initiatives, talkative employees who constantly try to engage other coworkers in conversation and so prevent them from getting their work done. Think about it; what do we say when a person becomes a constant source of irritation to us?" Neumann took one hand off the wheel to gesture in my direction.

"Huh? I'm sorry," I apologized. "What did you say?"

"We say, 'Stop being a pest.'[4] Where do you think this phrase came from?" Neumann asked.

"I have a pretty good idea," I said.

"Same principle. Often it's the smallest disturbance that makes our pasture an untenable place."

"My guess is," I replied, "there's not a lot we can do about that but try our best to minimize them." *And next time, I do the driving,* I thought.

"Right," Neumann replied. "But don't go overboard on it or you'll be sending out memos outlawing courtesy flushes in the bathroom."

When he finally slowed down to enter the Austin city limits, Neumann said, "Sheep will not lie down unless they are free from fear, rivalry, pests . . . and hunger. Like sheep, we also hunger, but for different things. The people who will report to you will sometimes hunger for more responsibility or advancement, at times for more pay. The point of making your pasture a safe place for your flock is that if you don't—"

"They'll search for one that is," I interrupted.

"Exactly. Companies often spend millions of dollars on training new people because the old ones become frustrated and move on to find greener pastures. The greener-grass syndrome not only ties up a tremendous amount of capital, but it puts an inevitable drag on productivity as we wait for newcomers to come up to speed. The problem can't be eliminated, of course. Some people are career vagabonds and will move on after a couple of years, no matter what their managers do. Companies might find out, however, that if they spent more resources on the back end of their personnel function, they might not have to spend so much on the front end."

At last, as he pulled in to the campus parking lot, Neumann said, "Ted, I know we've covered a lot today, but I wouldn't be a good teacher if I let you hop out without telling you two of the most important, practical principles about making your pasture at General Technologies a safe place where your people can thrive."

"Okay," I said, grateful that the car had come to a complete stop.

"Number one," Neumann said, "be visible. Don't be an absentee shepherd. What I've tried to tell you today is that you set the tone for the work environment of your department. If you create a safe place where your people can work in an undistracted atmosphere, you'll be amazed at what they can accomplish. You'll also be amazed at the loyalty you'll engender from your people. And you can't do that unless you get out and let your people see you. Nothing reassures the sheep more than the presence of the shepherd."

"If they trust the shepherd," I added. "That's why we talked first about how a leader creates a bond of trust between himself and his people."

Neumann looked at me and smiled. "The sheep will feel the protection of their leader if they instinctively know he has their best welfare at heart and can see that he's present in the field with them," he stated. "People are the same way. People can handle the uncertainty of tomorrow if they can see a leader they are certain they can trust today."

"That's great," I said, making copious notes in my journal.

"That's the first thing. The second thing comes from years of experience in doing it the wrong way."

"What's that?" I laughed.

"Don't give problems time to fester," Neumann said. "One of the things we kept coming back to today is the flocking instinct of sheep. In flocks I've led, I've seen many times how one sick sheep infected the entire group."

"You think that happened with the flock we saw today?" I asked.

"In all likelihood," Neumann answered. "A more attentive shepherd would have caught the problem sooner and dealt with it. You be sure and do that when you get to GT! If you act soon enough, an individual problem won't become a flock problem."

I mulled over that last statement for a minute, then Dr. Neumann stuck his hand out. "Now go get some rest," he said. "I want you to do your best, too."

"Thanks," I said. "I think I'll take the phone off the hook when I get home."

"That's a great idea," he said. "I may do the same."

It had been a productive lesson. In the minutes after Dr. Neumann drove off, I sat on the curb in front of the Business School and finished writing out the day's notes:

THE WAY OF THE SHEPHERD

4. Make Your Pasture a Safe Place
    - Keep your people well informed.
    - Infuse *every* position with importance.
    - Cull chronic instigators from the flock.
    - Regularly rotate the sheep to fresh pastures.
    - Reassure the sheep by staying visible.
    - Don't give problems time to fester.

CHAPTER 5

The Staff of Direction

My next lesson took place in Dr. Neumann's office. His secretary had called to notify me of the professor's busy schedule and to ask if I would mind meeting him there. I told her, "No problem at all." I didn't mind being indoors. In Texas the summer starts early, and I was glad our lesson would be indoors for once, where we could enjoy the air conditioning.

I arrived a little early. While waiting for Dr. Neumann to show, I took a moment to poke around his office. It impressed me how clean and tidy everything seemed. It wasn't piled high with old journals, like many other university offices I had seen. His bookshelves seemed to be stuffed with every imaginable tome ever written on the subject of business and strategy. *He must not watch a lot of TV,* I caught myself thinking.

Next I scanned the walls, which were richly adorned with parchments, numerous awards, and several certificates of appreciation. Overwhelmed by Dr. Neumann's achievements, I started talking to myself out loud. "Undergrad at Stanford; MBA from Wharton; and a Ph.D. from Harvard! This guy doesn't watch *any* TV."

Pictures and memorabilia from around the world also dotted the room. "This guy's been around," I said. "I don't even know what half of these knickknacks are."

"These *knickknacks,* as you call them," Neumann said, "are my treasures from around the world." He shut the door behind him and continued. "Two of them represent one of the reasons I asked you to meet me here. The other reason was because I'm swamped grading end-of-term papers—including yours."

"I'm sorry," I said, clearing my throat. "Maybe I should have used a term other than knickknack."

"Don't worry about it," he said. Then he carefully lifted two sticks off of the wall and placed them on his desk. Walking around to the other side of his desk, Neumann handed me the longer of the two and sat down in his office chair. The stick was a little over five feet long and had a large curve on one end that resembled a question mark.

"Do you know what that is, Ted?"

"Looks like a walking stick," I replied.

"That is a very old shepherd's staff," he said.

"Cool," I said. "Where did you get it?"

"From England," he replied. "I spent a summer teaching at Oxford and picked it up over there. The staff you're holding is more than two hundred years old."

"Wow," I exclaimed, "that's older than our country."

"That's nothing," Neumann replied. "Sheep were actually domesticated as far back as eight thousand years ago. In fact, wool garments were worn in Babylon—the name means 'land of the wool'—as early as 4000 B.C."[1]

"Now, *that's* old," I said.

"The staff and rod," Neumann said, pointing to the short stick on the table, "were forerunners of the scepters used by ancient kings, which is most appropriate, since the rulers were called the shepherds of their people."

He looked at me and continued. "The point is, the lessons you're learning are ancient in origin. These same leadership truths helped powerful kings govern their people. They have been tested through the ages, Ted, and they *work*. Now, let's talk about how the staff is used. Do you know?"

"Well, I suppose it's a hiking stick for the shepherd as he traverses rough terrain," I answered.

"I know from personal experience that it's good for that," Neumann said, "but that isn't the main purpose of the staff."

"Okay," I said, feeling more intrigued. "What is its main purpose?"

"The staff, Ted, is the most important tool the shepherd has to lead his sheep." Neumann paused to let his comment sink in.

"You mean . . . this is a *leadership* tool?" I asked as I examined the stick in my hand.

"That's exactly what it is," Neumann declared. He leaned forward and suddenly got serious. "There are four leadership functions the staff helps the shepherd perform. Each function represents a responsibility inherent in what it means to be a shepherd-leader. Fail in these things, Ted, and you will have failed your flock."

"I understand," I said.

"First," Neumann said, "the staff represents your responsibility to direct your people.[2] A shepherd's first duty of the day is to lead his flock out of the fold to find fresh pasture.[3] So the shepherd not only needs to know the terrain and where to find the greener grass but also how to get the flock there. A skilled shepherd can do that. He can single-handedly move a flock of more than a hundred sheep over fairly large distances."

"That's incredible," I responded. "How can one person do that?"

Neumann smiled. "The art of leadership," he said. "He uses what's in your hand."

"The staff?" I replied.

"Yes. Like any animal with a herd mentality, a sheep will generally follow the sheep in front of it. So the shepherd can steer an entire flock by getting in front of the herd and using his staff to gently nudge the lead sheep in the direction the shepherd wants to go."

"I bet that's quite a sight," I said.

"It's quite a feeling," Neumann replied, "so long as you know where you're going. It's quite another feeling when you're leading a large flock of hungry and thirsty sheep and you're lost!"

"I would imagine it's not real good for the sheep, either," I added, with a little sarcasm.

"No, it's not," Neumann replied. "Remember that neglected flock we saw last week? They wouldn't have been in such poor shape had their shepherd moved them to fresh pasture. Instead, they kept feeding on infected ground."[4]

"Sorry," I said, trying to get serious again. (It occurred to me that Neumann had yet to grade my term paper.)

"Don't worry about it," Neumann said. "The thing about sheep is they have a tendency to focus on the grass that's right in front of them. Therefore, someone has to keep an eye on where the flock is going.

"It works the same way with people. They tend to put their head down to do their work and don't look up again until the day is over. So someone has to keep an eye on the horizon to see where the green grass is. That person also has to keep the flock together and lead it where it needs to go. In a small finance department at General Technologies, that person will be you. Be a good shepherd and steer your flock. Know where you're going, get out in front, and keep your flock on the move."

He paused to let me soak in his counsel, then continued. "Now, when steering your flock, be sure you don't confuse the staff for the rod." He pointed to the second stick on the table. "Oftentimes leaders fail to win the loyalty of their people because they lead with the rod rather than the staff."

"Explain that," I said. "I think I know what you're talking about, but I want to hear more."

"For the most part," Neumann explained, "the staff is the gentler instrument of the two. The shepherd uses it to direct his flock with nudges and taps, not heavy-handed swings. As a result, his sheep follow him out of trust rather than fear."

"I get it," I said. "I've seen it the other way. You remember the boss I told you about who constantly pounded us in the ground when we did something wrong?"

"Yes," Neumann answered.

"He's a good example of someone who leads with the rod rather than the staff."

"That's right," Neumann agreed. "And how much loyalty did you feel for him as your leader?"

"None at all," I said. "We couldn't stand him. In fact, we were all afraid of him."

"That's why you worked for him, because you were afraid *not* to," he replied. "The shepherd leads his sheep. It's the barking dog that drives them."

I took a deep breath and said, "I would hate for my people to ever feel that way about me. So how do I provide direction for them so they feel like I'm their shepherd and not a barking dog?"

"With gentle taps and not hard swings," Neumann answered. "First, when directing your people, use persuasion, not coercion.[5] Instead of making pronouncements, make requests. Offer suggestions and ideas. Don't dictate and demand; instead, advocate and recommend.

"Second, point the way by getting out in front of your people and *showing* them the way. And when people do mess up, rather than pound them into the ground, like your boss did, use the incident as a teaching opportunity."

"That's a good word," I said.

"Thanks," he said, "now let's keep going. The second function of the staff is to establish boundaries. Even though sheep have tremendous flocking instincts, they also have a tendency to stray from the herd."

"That doesn't make sense," I objected. "How can they have a tendency to do something that goes against their instincts?"

"They don't mean to stray, Ted," Neumann explained. "They have their heads down, preoccupied with eating grass. The problem is, sheep can see only about fifteen yards ahead. If they get pointed in a direction that's different than the one the flock is moving in, they don't have to nibble far before they're completely lost."

"I'm not sure I'm liking this comparison between sheep and people," I said. "It's starting to make me feel like an idiot."

Neumann laughed. "Haven't you ever made decisions in your life, seemingly insignificant at the time, and then looked up later and said, 'How in the world did I ever end up over here?'"

"Yes," I said. "More times than I like to admit."

"Well, if the shoe fits . . ."

"Okay, I get the picture," I said. "Let's get back to the sheep."

"Actually," he replied, "let's get back to the shepherd. It's his responsibility to keep the sheep together and pointed in the same direction. If he sees that a sheep is headed away from the safety of the herd, he'll take the straight end of his staff and tap the sheep on its far shoulder as a signal that it's headed in the wrong direction. If the sheep doesn't get the message, he'll slip the curved end of the staff around its neck and physically pull the sheep into alignment with the rest of the flock."

Neumann noticed my slightly puzzled look and continued, "That staff isn't long because it's a walking stick; it's long to extend the reach of the shepherd. When you get to General Technologies, it will be your responsibility to make sure all your people know where the fence line is. If they go beyond it, it's your responsibility to give them a tap on the shoulder."

"And if that doesn't work?" I asked.

"You ratchet it up a notch," Neumann replied. "Establishing boundaries isn't a matter of ego; it's a matter of practicality and safety. Your department can't fulfill its mission unless everyone acts together. What's more, you can't protect anyone who has strayed beyond the safety of your reach. Boundaries aren't bad things; they're good things. Unless, of course, you confuse boundaries with bridles."

"In other words," I said, "make sure my people know where the fence line is but give them freedom of movement within it."

"Exactly!" Neumann replied. "We bridle horses because we ride them. We don't ride sheep. One of the biggest mistakes new managers make is to micromanage their people. They think that teamwork means that everyone has to do everything the same way. Ted, you want to make sure your people don't get too far ahead of you, but you don't want them to feel like they're incarcerated, either. You provide direction and set expectations, then let your people decide how best to get there. If they stray too far, give them a tap to let them know it."

"Or ratchet it up," I said.

"Or ratchet it up," Neumann repeated.

"This is a pretty amazing stick," I said as I stood up with the staff. I began to move it around as if I knew how to use it. "There's much more to it than meets the eye. What other two functions does it serve?"

"It's a *staff*," Neumann said, watching me from across the desk with a slightly amused look. "And yes, it can do a lot in the hands of a skilled shepherd."

"Like what else?"

"Third, the staff helps the shepherd to rescue stranded sheep."

"Stranded sheep?" I asked.

"Yes. Because no matter how great a shepherd you are or how hard you try, occasionally a sheep will stray from the flock. Remember the first day I introduced you to my sheep?"

"How could I forget?" I said.

"What was the first thing I asked you to do?"

I thought back and replied, "You asked me to count the sheep."

"Right," Neumann said, "very good. I wanted to make sure no one was missing. There have been times that I've come up short because a sheep or two found a weak spot in the fence and crawled through."

"What did you do then?" I asked.

"I went looking for them." Neumann answered. "I've told you, sheep are pretty vulnerable creatures. A lot of bad things can happen to them when they stray beyond the pasture."

"You mean predators?" I wondered.

"That, and they can get stuck in positions they can't get out of. I've seen strays get stuck in rock crevices, and others who have gotten their thick wool so entangled in the underbrush that they can't move.[6] If I don't find them quickly, they can easily dehydrate or, as you said, become easy pickings for predators. So when my sheep get in trouble, I take my staff and go looking for them. Once I find them, I use the curved end of the staff to pull them out. Sometimes I spend hours searching for a lost sheep."

"What if it's raining?" I probed.

"Doesn't matter. They're *my* sheep. I'm responsible for their well-being and safety. If they're in trouble, I go out and get them."

I'll bet people loved working for you, I thought to myself. I began looking at Neumann with a growing appreciation.

"Works the same way with people," he said. "No matter how hard you try to keep everyone together and headed in the right direction, some people are still going to wander off and get in trouble. It happens without fail. It's happened everywhere I've ever been." Neumann shook his head. "When that happens to you, Ted—when a member of your flock at GT gets in trouble—you go and get them out!"

"What kind of trouble are you talking about?" I asked.

"They'll surprise you every time," Neumann said. "Sometimes you'll be amazed at their ingenuity at getting into trouble. Maybe they've screwed up an order, ticked off a vendor, alienated an important customer, or overstepped their bounds. It's up to you as their shepherd to get them out of trouble. When you do, you'll be amazed at their loyalty to you and the trust they'll place in you."

My head began to swim with all the lessons a simple stick was teaching me. And yet we weren't quite through.

"Finally," Neumann said, "let's talk about the fourth leadership responsibility the staff represents."

"Okay," I said, again taking my seat and laying the staff on Neumann's desk.

"The staff represents the shepherd's responsibility to encourage his flock," he declared.

"I don't doubt the need for that," I said, "but how does the shepherd encourage with a stick?"

"With a *staff*," Neumann corrected.

"I mean, the staff," I said.

"In a couple of different ways. Sometimes the shepherd uses it to separate a sheep from the rest of the flock and pull it in close to him. At other times he uses the staff to gently stroke the side or back of a sheep. It's a signal to let a sheep know that it's been noticed by the shepherd."

"Why would they need to know that? I asked.

"For comfort," he replied. "Don't forget that nothing reassures the sheep more than the presence of the trusted shepherd. I remember one time growing up when I was out on the range and a dog attacked one of our ewes. I made it there in time, but she still got scratched up pretty badly. For the next several days, wherever I led the flock, I had her walk next to me so she could feel my protection. It was my way of letting her know that I was there to support her. For months after that incident, long after she had healed, she would come up to me and rub her head against my leg."

Neumann turned his gaze on me and continued. "Good shepherds don't forget to encourage their people now and again, Ted. There'll be times when the best leadership you can provide is to pull a scratched-up employee next to you and let him feel your support. Maybe he got mixed up and made a horrendous bookkeeping error; whatever the case, that's the time when your employee needs to have his confidence restored.[7] All it will take is a stroke or two from you to let him know that failure isn't fatal in Ted McBride's department. Do that, and you'll be a shepherd your sheep will want to follow."

"Now," he said as he took the staff over to its spot on his office wall, "do you have any more questions?"

"No," I replied. "This has been really good. I think you've given me more than enough to think about."

"And I have more than enough papers to grade," he replied as he placed the staff back onto its mount and stepped back to admire it. "Not too bad for a *knickknack*."

Later that night I reviewed the day's notes on what it means for a shepherd to carry the staff of leadership. Here's what I took away from my latest lesson:

THE WAY OF THE SHEPHERD

5. The Staff of Direction
   - Know where you're going, get out in front, and keep your flock on the move.
   - When directing, use persuasion rather than coercion.
   - Give your people freedom of movement, but make sure they know where the fence line is. Don't confuse boundaries with bridles!
   - When your people get in trouble, go and get them out.
   - Remind your people that failure isn't fatal.

CHAPTER 6

The Rod of Correction

As graduation day approached, I sensed that my time with Dr. Neumann was drawing to a close. I had learned many lessons over the last several weeks that I knew would stay with me for the rest of my life.

I had learned that every attribute of great leadership is embodied in the life and work of the shepherd. I also noticed that Jack Neumann modeled the principles he was teaching me. This man practiced what he preached! Those of us in his classes knew how demanding he could be; he refused to accept any work but our very best. (Most of our papers came back with so many red marks and comments that it looked as if Dr. Neumann had bled over them.) But, to the last of us, we also knew he was 100 percent committed to us as "his" students. He, more than anyone else, wanted us to succeed.

I had come to look forward to our times together. It made me feel important to have an opportunity to interact with this great man outside of the classroom. While I doggedly looked forward to graduation and a release from the intense scholastic grind, I also knew I would greatly miss these unique encounters with Jack Neumann.

I was pretty sure I knew what the topic of our next lesson would be. We met Saturday morning around 10:00 A.M. at the intramural fields. The place was deserted. With finals only a few days away, students were either studying or catching up on much-needed sleep.

"Hello, Ted." Neumann said as he walked onto the field.

"Hello, Dr. Neumann," I answered, immediately noticing the short club he was carrying. I had seen it in his office the week before. "I have a feeling I know what that is," I said.

"This is an *iwisi*," Neumann replied.

"An *i-what?*" I said.

"An *iwisi*. It goes by different names. That's what they call it in Africa. Shepherds and Zulu warriors used it. In Ireland it is called a *knobkerrie*. In the Middle East it is a *shebet*. We know it as a shepherd's rod. Regardless of continent of origin, it's made pretty much the same way," he explained as he handed it to me.

I turned the club in my hands so I could get a better look at it. It was about eighteen inches long, smooth to the grip, and heavily weighted on one end by a large knob or ball.

"It's a root cut out of the ground," Neumann said. "The knob on the end is the bulb or a large knot in the root. That's what makes this thing such a fierce weapon. It's also what gives it its sailing ability."

"Sailing ability?" I asked. "What do you mean?"

Neumann grabbed the *knobkerrie* out of my hands, and with a hard swing, he heaved the club into the air. It arced across the sky toward the other end of the field. I couldn't believe how far the thing flew.

"Wow," I said. "That's incredible!"

"That's nothing," he replied. "You ought to see it in the hands of an African herdsman! Today, of course, we use rifles to protect our herds, but in some parts of the world, shepherds still use these. They can hurl them across a plain with pinpoint accuracy. In the hands of a skilled shepherd, an *iwisi* can be deadly."

He gestured for me to walk with him over to where the rod had landed and said, "Last week we talked about the staff and how it's used in the hands of a skilled shepherd to guide his flock. We also talked about your responsibility as a shepherd to direct your flock at General Technologies."

"I remember," I said. "You spoke of using persuasion rather than coercion and about giving people freedom of movement but making sure they know where the fence line is. You also told me that when my people get in trouble, it's my responsibility to go and get them out." I repeated the whole spiel because I wanted my teacher to know that I remembered.

"That's good," he said, "thank you."

Once more he fixed his eyes on the *iwisi* and said, "Today, we're going to talk about a necessary part of leadership that's not so enjoyable."

"Bearing the rod," I interrupted.

"That's right," he agreed. "The staff represents your responsibility to direct your people; the rod represents your responsibility to correct them. This is the part of leadership that leaders, particularly new ones, most commonly err on. If you use the rod too much or incorrectly, you'll lose the goodwill of your people. Use it too little or not at all, and you'll lose their respect. You can't be a shepherd who engenders the loyalty and trust of his people, Ted, if you don't get this right."

When we arrived at the *iwisi*'s landing spot, Neumann bent down and picked it up. He held it up between us and said, "You've got to know when to use this and how. Wield this fairly and wisely, and your people will respect you and love you for it. Use it poorly, and they'll look for another shepherd. Let's sit down and talk."

We took our impromptu seats, and Neumann continued the lesson. "The rod," he said, "like the staff, is an extension of the shepherd's arm. The shepherd uses the rod for three things.[1] First, he wields the rod to protect his sheep from predators."

"What kind of predators?" I asked.

"Well, it depends on the region," Neumann replied. "Usually animals like coyotes, wild dogs, wolves, occasionally a mountain lion."

"You mean, attack a mountain lion with *this?*" I asked with more than a hint of incredulity. "I imagine a shepherd would have to get in pretty close to use it." I noticed once more how short the club looked.

"That's an astute observation," Neumann said with a smile. "Sometimes shepherds also carried slings and rocks. If the slingshot didn't scare the animal away, however, the shepherd had only his *shebet* to defend his flock. I can guarantee you, Ted, back when a shepherd cut this rod out from beneath an oak tree, he knew he was carving a weapon of last resort. When predators came down from the hills, hungry for the taste of mutton, the only thing that stood between them and their dinner was a rod-wielding shepherd."

"Isn't that dangerous?" I said. "I mean, for the shepherd."

"Yes, and scary too, but that's what a good shepherd does. He stands in the gap for his sheep. That's what you'll do for your flock at General Technologies, if you're a good shepherd. I'm betting that you will be."

"I appreciate that," I said. "But what do you mean?"

"I mean there'll be times at GT when your flock feels threatened. Sometimes they will feel endangered by circumstances. More often than not, it will be due to an aggressor. Trust me, there will be times when someone will be screaming for a member of your flock's head. I know this sounds a bit foreign to you now, but just wait."

Neumann's eyes seemed to drift to another time. In a few moments, he continued, "I remember one time, long before I came to UT, I was responsible for a department that did risk analysis. We evaluated deals in the works to see if they presented too much financial risk for the company. Problem was, the deals didn't originate in our department. They came from another area of the company. So our job was to say yea or nay to someone else's pet project. When a member of my team rejected a deal that represented seven months of a certain man's time—and a good deal of his performance bonus, I might add—the fellow blew his stack."

"What happened?" I asked.

"He came charging into our department like a mad dog," Neumann said. "He got in the face of a member of *my* flock and started screaming in her face. You've never heard such profanity! Not only was she publicly humiliated, but she felt more than a little exposed. He was about three grades her senior."

"What did *you* do?" I asked.

"I showed her I was a shepherd worthy of her trust. I was Johnny-on-the-spot. I stepped right into the middle of the fray. One second he was looking at her; the next second he was looking at me."

"Did that stop him?" I asked.

"Not at first. He just kept screaming, this time at me. That's what I wanted, of course. I was determined to take the heat for a member of my flock. This man was way out of line. After he calmed down a little, we retreated to my office, and I used my *knobkerrie* on him."

"How so?"

"I let him know, in no uncertain terms, that if he had a problem he couldn't peacefully resolve with a member of my flock, he was to come to me. It didn't take terribly long before people in the company learned that offensive behavior directed toward someone in my flock would earn them a face-to-face encounter with me. Of course, there were times, over the years, when people had valid complaints against members of my flock. When that occurred, I took the blame and then went to the erring individual and worked out the problem privately."

"Your people had to appreciate you for that," I said.

"They did," Neumann agreed. "It gave them a measure of security. They felt less vulnerable knowing that I was around to protect them."

"I've never had an opportunity to work for someone like that," I admitted sadly. "The manager I worked for *never* went to bat for us. If we failed to meet our profit objectives, he would blame us to his superiors and then turn around and blame his superiors to us for 'their lack of leadership.'"

"That stinks," Neumann said. "What a poor excuse for a leader! Nothing saps *esprit de corps* more than a namby-pamby leader who tries to play both sides of the fence. Ted, when you get to General Technologies, remember that when your people feel attacked, they need to know they have a shepherd they can depend on who will stand in the gap and fight for *them*. Do that, and your people will love you. What's more, if you stand up for your people, they'll stand up for you when it's *your* head someone wants on a platter."

As I began to visualize the scene, Neumann changed direction. "Now let's shift gears," he said. "The *knobkerrie* has other uses besides protecting the sheep from predators. Shepherds often use it to protect the sheep from themselves."

"From themselves?" I said. "Why would a shepherd have to protect a sheep from itself?"

"Because sheep often don't know what's for their own good," he replied. "As a result, they sometimes put themselves in danger."

"That's pretty dumb," I said. "I know sheep aren't the smartest animals, but you'd think they would at least know what's good for them."

Neumann shot me a blank look. "Ted, haven't you ever made a bad decision that could have ended up hurting you?"

I didn't have to ponder the question for long. "You mean, like leaving Phoenix in the rain at ten o'clock at night, driving over a thousand miles for twenty hours straight, just so I could see my girlfriend in Dallas as early as possible?" I asked.

"Yes."

"No, I've never done that," I lied. "Let's get back to the sheep."

Neumann chuckled and said, "When the shepherd notices a sheep about to do something that could jeopardize its safety, or that of the flock, he uses the rod as an instrument of discipline. If a shepherd looks up and sees that a sheep is wandering away on its own or is about to eat a poisonous plant, for example, he'll hurl the rod toward the erring animal to send it scampering back to the flock or away from the harmful plant."[2]

"I thought you mentioned last week that the shepherd was to use the staff to rescue a lost sheep," I said, thinking how a smack from the *knobkerrie* would smart.

"I did, and you're right," Neumann said. "A good shepherd does his best to keep his sheep from getting into trouble in the first place. But if a sheep wanders too far off the beaten path, it is beyond the immediate reach of the shepherd's staff. If the sheep is still within the shepherd's sight, the kindest thing he can do is to set sail with the rod and send a message to the sheep to return to the safety of the flock."

I nodded and Neumann continued. "There's another reason shepherds occasionally use the rod rather than the staff," he said. "You'll understand this better after you get to General Technologies."

"And what's that?" I asked.

"Some animals require the shepherd to speak in a louder voice. Sheep can be stubborn, rebellious creatures. Every now and then, you'll find a truly obstinate member of your flock will require you to use a bit more persuasion than the other sheep in your fold.

"In the end, however, it doesn't really matter whether the sheep is unruly or well intended. Throughout your managerial career, Ted, there will be times when you'll look up and notice that a member of your flock has strayed well beyond the safety zone. Your vantage point as shepherd will allow you to look ahead and see dangers he can't see. You'll instinctively know that if he continues in that direction, he's bound for trouble. When that happens, a gentle nudge of the staff won't do; it's time for you to step in and use the rod."

"That sounds painful," I said.

"But it's better for the sheep to endure momentary pain than to have its well-being put in jeopardy," Neumann replied.

"I wasn't talking about the sheep," I said. "I was talking about me."

"Very funny," Neumann said.

"I'm not just trying to be funny," I explained. "I can't imagine anything more uncomfortable than having to discipline someone."

"Well," he said, "part of the reason you feel uncomfortable with the idea is that you don't fully understand it. There are a lot of misconceptions out there about the purpose of discipline. It's not about putting someone in their place or about beating the sheep to death. It's not about giving them one last chance or cuffing their hands."

"What is it about, then?" I asked.

"It's about a course correction. It's about sitting down with that person privately and saying, 'Hey, there's a bridge out ahead, and I don't want you to get hurt.' You see? You discipline your people, not to harm them, but to keep them from harm."

"I can appreciate that," I said. "But to be honest, I've been on the receiving end of a disciplinary talk a time or two, and it certainly felt harmful to me."

"The key," Neumann explained, "is to guide the person in a course correction without alienating them, and *that* depends on how you approach the conversation."

"Okay, so how do I approach it?"

"You approach the conversation as a teaching opportunity," Neumann replied. "In fact, the Latin word for 'discipline' is *discipulus*—"

Oh, great, I thought. *I'm one week away from finals, and he's using Latin on me!*

"—from which we get the word 'pupil.' Get it? Discipline isn't about handing out punishment or assigning blame; it's about instruction. It's about instructing your people in the direction they should go by helping them see further down the path they're currently treading. That's far different than calling someone in because they 'fouled up.' In the final analysis, when the shepherd throws the rod at an errant sheep, it shows that he's looking out for it."

"I see, now that you put it that way," I said, "but what if the person I'm disciplining doesn't buy it?"

Neumann gave me a thoughtful smile. "They'll buy it, Ted—if they buy *you*."

I thought about his comment for several moments. "I hope they will," I said, more to myself than to Dr. Neumann.

"If you've been a shepherd to them, they will, Ted. If you've used the rod to *protect* them, I guarantee they'll be more inclined to listen and respect you when you use it to *correct* them."

"Are you saying it won't hurt them as much?" I asked.

"I'm not saying your discipline won't hurt them," Neumann said. "Let's face it, no one likes to be told they don't know where they're going. I am saying, however, that when they know the message is coming from someone who has their best interest at heart, they're much more likely to receive the discipline as coming from a trusted friend. But you have to show them, first, that you *are* trustworthy."

Neumann let that idea sink in for a moment, then continued. "Come on," he said, "let's head back, and I'll tell you about the third use of the rod."

As we walked together back to the parking lot, Neumann got ready to deliver on his promise. "Okay," he said, "first, the rod represents your responsibility to *protect*. Second, it represents your responsibility to *correct*. Third, it represents your responsibility to *inspect*.

"Last week, Ted, when we talked about the staff and the responsibilities it represented, I told you that the shepherd's first duty of the day is to lead his flock out of the fold to find fresh pasture. Remember?"

"Yes," I replied.

"Well, at the end of the day, it is the shepherd's responsibility to billet his sheep in a safe place for the night. This might be a cave or a pen the shepherd constructed. The shepherd then stands at the entrance of the fold and counts the sheep as they enter."

"Let me guess," I said. "He counts the sheep with the rod."

"That's exactly right," Neumann said. "In ancient days it was called 'passing under the rod.' Not only would the shepherd count the sheep to make sure they were all accounted for, but he would often use the rod to part the wool on the sheep so he could more closely inspect them. You see, the longer a sheep's wool grows, the more difficult it is for the shepherd to detect any health problems the wool might be hiding. Surely you've heard the phrase 'Don't let him pull the wool over your eyes'?"

"Of course," I said.

"That's where the phrase comes from," Neumann said. "If you're going to shepherd your people at General Technologies, you have to regularly check on their progress. You have to part the wool, so to speak, and take a good look at how they're doing. I've already told you how a sick or lame sheep will do everything it can to avoid being singled out by a predator?"

"Yes."

"It works the same way with people," Neumann said. "I can't tell you the number of times I've seen a group of people huddling around a conference table to receive instructions on how to do something. They all sit there, nodding their heads like they understand. Then the next thing you know, they're privately going back and forth to one another, trying to figure out what was said. Everyone was nodding their head, but no one wanted to spill the beans that they didn't get it.

"It's your duty," Neumann continued, "to regularly inquire about the progress of your people, because *you're* responsible for developing them."

"Do you have any suggestions on how I should go about that?" I asked.

"I think it's something you learn as you go along," he replied. "It's not hard if you'll just take the time to do it. Periodically call your people in and ask how they're doing. Ask them if there is anything you can help them with, anything they need clarification on. You can say all day long, 'Come to me if you have any problems,' but chances are the members of your flock who need help the most will be the ones who are least likely to ask for it. They're just like that lame sheep that does everything it can to blend in with the flock. Don't forget, Ted, it's *your* job, not theirs, to part the wool."

As I let his words sink in, he spoke again. "One other thing, while we're at it," he said.

"What's that?" I asked.

"If a person never indicates they need help when you inquire about their progress, it means either that they don't trust you enough to be honest with you or that you haven't sufficiently challenged them to grow. If it's the latter, you need to look harder for projects you can put in front of your people that will develop them. People who aren't progressively increasing in their capabilities have a shepherd who's stunting their growth. You need to wield the rod of inspection to make sure that doesn't happen."

"You said, 'If it's the latter,'" I replied. "What if it's the former?"

Neumann put his arm around me as we walked off the field. "You do the things we've talked about the last several weeks," he declared, "and you won't have to worry about your people not trusting or following you. Now let's get back to school. I have a final exam to write."

"Now, *that's* painful," I said.

"Yes, it can be," Neumann grinned. "But it's how *I* pull the wool back to inspect *your* progress."

"Gee, thanks," I said. "Any suggestions on how I should prepare for your exam?" I hoped to glean some tidbit of information that would give me an edge.

"Yes," Neumann replied. "You need to study everything we've talked about from the first day of class to the last."

"Great, thanks for the clarification," I said. "I really appreciate it."

"My pleasure. By the way, what are your plans for next Saturday night?"

"After finals? I don't have any plans. Collapse, I suppose."

"Well, we don't want you to do that, but Mrs. Neumann and I would like you to join us for dinner around five."

I grinned, nodded my head, and agreed to the plan. It sounded perfect.

That night before I began studying, I looked at my notes on the Way of the Shepherd. They were beginning to fill out. I added notes on what I had learned from Dr. Neumann earlier that day:

THE WAY OF THE SHEPHERD

6. The Rod of Correction
   - *Protect:* Stand in the gap and fight for your sheep.
   - *Correct:* Approach discipline as a teaching opportunity.
   - *Inspect:* Regularly inquire about your people's progress.

CHAPTER 7

THE HEART OF THE SHEPHERD

The sun had sunk low in the late afternoon sky by dinnertime. I couldn't have been more tired or exuberant—tired because I had just gone through finals, exuberant because they were over. After two years of hard work, thousands of tuition dollars, countless lectures, and untold hours of lost sleep spent writing case studies, solving problems, and preparing for exams, my MBA education had finally come to an end. Graduation was only two days away. I had done it!

What surprised me was the touch of melancholy I felt. Never again would my classmates and I gather in the ways we had over the past two years. It's said that war makes strange bedfellows. I suppose it's true. My classmates had come from every region of the world, every strata of society, yet a strong bond had grown between us. We had survived a grueling program. What's more, we had done it together.

My sense of fulfillment and loss over the life I had lived those two years was partially offset that night by the honor accorded me by Dr. Jack Neumann and his wife. Every student knows that much of the closeness they feel with their teacher in the give-and-take of the classroom is false. The interactions are real but limited to the academic environs. University professors are public figures who lead private lives. To be invited into the home of one, therefore, is to be allowed into the inner sanctum. I counted it a great privilege to be allowed into Jack Neumann's home, for I could name no one whom I admired or respected more.

We enjoyed a splendid meal that evening out on the veranda. Afterward Dr. Neumann and I sipped our after-dinner coffee and ruminated on what had been and what was to come.

"Congratulations on your achievement," Dr. Neumann said to me. "You've done a great job. I'm proud of you."

"Thanks," I replied. "There are a lot of things I'm proud of tonight. I'm proud to have been admitted to, and now to graduate from, one of the top MBA programs in the country. I'm proud to have been counted among my classmates, proud that I did well. But I think one of the things I'm the most proud of, Dr. Neumann, is to have taken a seat in your class."

"Thanks, Ted," he said. "That's awfully nice of you to say. I was glad to have you there."

"And another thing," I said, "I'm glad I was smart enough to take you up on your offer and give you my Saturdays."

We sat for a few moments in silence, enjoying the kind of satisfaction that comes only when teacher and student have completed their work together.

"It's amazing," I finally said.

"What's amazing?" Neumann asked.

"That it's over. I can hardly believe it. It seems like only yesterday I was sitting in class for the first time, wondering what in the world I had gotten myself into and questioning whether I could hack it. Now it's all over." I stared at the floor.

Neumann stood up and thumped his coffee mug on the table. "Well, Mr. McBride," he said, "you may have completed your MBA program, but you haven't completed *my* program. Not yet, anyway. You still have one more lesson to learn."

"You've got to be kidding," I said, with the most deadpan face I could muster.

"No, I'm not kidding," he answered. "Besides, it was getting a tad too syrupy just then. Let's take a walk and check out the sheep."

Neumann's ranch house sat atop a large hill that overlooked his land and the prized flock of sheep he kept on the far hillside below. The sheep calmly grazing on lush, green pasture beside the still water of the nearby pond made for a picturesque walk and a beautiful backdrop for the last, and most important, conversation we were to have on the Way of the Shepherd.

"Ted," Neumann said, "I've enjoyed sharing with you what I've learned about leadership, but there is one thing we haven't talked about."

"What's that?" I said.

"The cost. This approach to leadership comes with a high price tag for the leader."

"What kind of price tag?" I asked.

"Your time, your commitment, your personal energy and involvement. It will cost you yourself, Ted. You aren't learning a set of management techniques but an outlook. More than anything, the Way of the Shepherd is a lifestyle of leadership that places great value on the worth of the flock.

"If you're going to be that type of leader, Ted—if you're going to shepherd your people at General Technologies—then you need to know there's a huge cost involved. It will cost you to get your people out of trouble when they wander off. It will cost you emotionally to wield the rod and to sometimes inflict pain on your people. You'll have to do things you won't particularly feel like doing at the time."

Neumann shook his head to emphasize his next point. "Great leadership is hard work," he said. "More than that, it's unrelenting. Those who do it well do so because they are willing to pay the price. You need to know that going in."

"I understand," I said.

"I hope so," he replied. "Because if you're not willing to pay the price, your people will end up paying."

"What do you mean?" I asked.

Thinking back for a moment, Neumann said, "You remember that pitiful flock we saw a few weeks ago?"

"Yes," I said.

"The sheep didn't have a shepherd who was willing to pay the price to be who he was supposed to be. So the sheep ended up paying for his poor leadership. That's what I'm talking about. *Someone* has to pay; it's just a matter of who will pay. The thing is it's not the sheep who get to decide. That decision is made by the one who tends the flock. So every day when you go to work at General Technologies, *you* get to decide who's going to pay for your leadership that day—you or your people."

Neumann looked me straight in the eye and asked, "Ted, do you know why that man wasn't willing to pay the price?"

"Evidently he thought the cost was too high," I answered.

"Yes and no," Neumann replied. "Remember microeconomics? The price you're willing to pay is relative to the value you attribute to something. That man refused to pay the price, not because he thought it was too high but because the value he put on his sheep was too low. Shepherds call a person like that a 'hireling.'"

"A hireling?" I repeated. "What's that?"

"A hireling is person who tends the flock only because it's a job," he explained. "The sheep mean nothing more to someone like that than an opportunity to get paid. If you're looking for the difference between me and the other man and why I'm willing to pay a price that he is not, there it is. He tends sheep for the money. I do it because I love the sheep, and that makes all the difference."

We both grew quiet as we considered this last profound statement. Then Neumann spoke up again. "Over the last several weeks," he said, "we've talked a lot about what it means to shepherd a flock of people. Ted, what I want you to know is this: What makes a shepherd a shepherd isn't the staff or the rod; it's the heart. What distinguishes a great leader from a mediocre one is that a great leader has a heart for his people."

"I don't disagree with that," I said. "But what does that mean exactly?"

"How you view your people determines how you lead them," Neumann replied. "If you don't have a heart for your people, you'll look at them differently than someone who does. You'll see them as expenses and interruptions, and you'll never invest yourself in them like a shepherd would. You may talk a good game, even play a good game for a while, but you won't have the drive to do all the things we've talked about over the last several weeks. You'll do just what that hireling did. You'll eventually count the cost as too high, focus on nothing but the work, and leave your people to fend for themselves."

Just about that time we reached the flock. The sheep paid little attention to us as we walked through the gate; they were too busy grazing. Neumann poked me in the ribs with his elbow and said, "Watch this!" He gave out a low, guttural call. As if by magic, the sheep came to him from every corner of the field. Neumann bent down and began petting the sheep. He ran his hands over their ears, patted them on their heads, and scratched their sides. It amazed me (but by this point, it didn't surprise me) to learn that he had named each sheep. "Hello Black Foot!" he called out. "Hi Brown Ear!"[1]

Over the last several weeks I had come to understand the special relationship Neumann had with these animals. Recalling that first Saturday, I felt more than a little embarrassed that I had referred to Dr. Neumann's flock as "stinking sheep." I also realized that on that day I had viewed the sheep as an interruption to my training and time. I knew, of course, that sheep aren't people, but I also knew it was a part of my personality to get so focused on the task at hand that I could easily view an employee as an interruption. And that bothered me.

I watched Dr. Neumann interacting with his flock. They obviously enjoyed one another. One thing I knew for sure: Jack Neumann was no hireling. He loved these animals!

He looked up and caught my eye. "So what do you think?" he asked.

"Pretty impressive," I replied. "How do you do that?"

Neumann stood up. "You make the call on the back of your tongue. Like this . . ." Once again he lowered his head slightly and emitted a very throaty *"Tahhoo."*[2]

"That doesn't seem too hard," I said.

"Why don't you give it a try?" Neumann suggested.

"No, I couldn't do that," I replied. "I'd feel way too self-conscious."

"Well, don't," Neumann ordered. "Every shepherd has his call. That's the one my sheep respond to. Give it a try. You can do it."

"Okay," I said. "But don't laugh."

"I won't, Ted. Go ahead."

I took a step or two back, bowed my head, and gave the best approximation I could of Neumann's call. *"Tahoo!"*

Neumann grinned and came over to me. "That was good, Ted," he said. "You pretty well nailed it. Would you like to try calling the sheep?"

"I'd love to!" I replied.

"All right, go to the other side of the field, put your back up against the fence, and give a good, clear yell that every sheep across the pasture can hear."

"Okay," I said. "I'll give it the old college try."

By this time I felt a bit more confident, but nevertheless I practiced the call under my breath all the way out to the fence line. I still felt unsure of myself and didn't want to fail in front of my teacher.

"All right," I said as I took my place.

"Go ahead, Ted."

"Tahhoo!" I called out with conviction.

The sheep just stood there.

"That's all right, Ted," Neumann called out. "Do it again."

"Okay," I said. *"Tahhoo!!"*

Still the sheep ignored me.

"You're doing great, Ted," Neumann shouted, even as he began walking my way for support. "Don't give up. This time do it a little deeper."

I nodded. *"Tahhhhoooo!"*

This time a couple of sheep looked in my direction.

Halfway to me, Neumann lifted his voice. "That's it, Ted. Now just do it a little louder."

I took a deep breath. *"Taaahhhooooo!!"*

Now several sheep turned their heads in my direction. Neumann stood right beside me and said, "I think you're almost there, Ted. Do it one more time."

"Okay," I replied, a little out of breath. *"Taaaahhhhooooo!!!"*

Virtually every sheep in the pasture turned and looked at me. Then, blinking a few times, they turned their heads back to the grass and began grazing again.

"They're not coming to me!" I said, crestfallen.

"No," Neumann whispered, "but I'm sure they found you extremely entertaining. I know I did."

He had tears in his eyes from laughter.

"Dr. Neumann, if I had a *knobkerrie* on me, I'd use it on you right now!" I was trying hard not to laugh myself.

Neumann wiped the tears from his eyes. "I'm sure going to miss our Saturdays together," he cackled, more to himself than to me.

"Well, I'm glad I could be the source of your amusement," I answered.

"Uh," he said, trying to catch his breath. "I shouldn't do that after eating such a big meal. My stomach hurts."

"I still don't get it," I said. "Why didn't they come? I gave the call as well as you did."

Neumann grinned from ear to ear. "You made that call better than I *ever* did," he said. "Matter of fact, I think you're probably the best sheep caller I've ever heard!"

"Cut it out," I said. "I'm serious. Why didn't they come to me the way they did to you?"

"All right," he replied. "As dumb as sheep can sometimes be, Ted, they're careful about who they answer to. It's a fact that sheep won't follow the call of a stranger."[3]

"And why's that?" I asked.

"Because they don't know if the stranger is someone they can trust. Ted, you could be the greatest shepherd in the world, but if they don't know you as *their* shepherd, you're just a stranger to them.

"There's an important principle here. The ultimate test of leadership isn't setting a direction for your flock. The ultimate test is this: can you get your flock where you want it to go? Ted, if your people at GT don't see you as their shepherd, they'll find it difficult to vest you with the trust they need to truly follow you. The reason these sheep came when I called, as opposed to you, is because they know they can trust me as their shepherd."

"I get it," I said. "By being a good shepherd to my people, I show them that I'm worthy of being followed."

"Exactly. Just like what we talked about in class. The quality of your return is based on the quality of your investment. If you want your people to return loyalty and trust to you, you first have to invest your loyalty and trust in them. That's why it's called a return. If you give your people halfhearted leadership, you'll get a halfhearted following. But if you invest yourself in them, if you have a heart for them, your people will return your investment with a heartfelt following."

Neumann gathered himself for a moment and then said, "If there's been a secret to my success, Ted, that's it. I made up my mind more than thirty years ago that I wasn't going to be a hireling or a stranger. I was going to be a shepherd. Several weeks ago you asked me to teach you what I knew about leading people. I've taught you what I've learned and what I know. Now it's up to you to choose what kind of a leader you're going to be."

"Dr. Neumann," I declared, "I'm going to be a shepherd."

Neumann smiled. "I know."

"I'm not going to be a hireling or a stranger," I insisted.

"No, Ted, I don't believe you will."

"Thanks," I said. "Dr. Neumann?"

"Yes?"

"How do you know I won't?" I asked.

"You remember standing in my office and asking me if I would teach you how to manage people?"

"Of course," I said.

"What did I tell you?" Neumann asked.

"You said I would have to give up all of my Saturdays until graduation."

"That's right. Part of the reason I told you that was out of practicality. I've been so busy that it was the only time I had. But what you didn't know, Ted, is that I was testing you. I wanted to know if you were willing to give up what little free time you had. If you weren't willing to pay the price to *learn* the Way of the Shepherd, I knew there was no way you'd pay the price to *practice* the Way of the Shepherd."

It was then that I realized how much Jack Neumann had invested in me. He had done far more than teach me the Way of the Shepherd. He had personally modeled it for me. A huge debt of gratitude began to well up inside of me. A man I looked up to and respected believed in *me*. I wanted to succeed at General Technologies for a whole host of reasons, but now one more got added to the list: I wanted to make Jack Neumann proud of me.

"I don't know how to thank you for everything you've done for me," I said.

"You don't need to thank me," Jack said. "I enjoyed every minute of it, especially the sheep-calling up the hill." He put his hand on my shoulder. "Ted, what you can do is give me a good return on my investment. Put into practice what you've learned here and pass it on to others along the way."

"I will," I said. "I promise."

The End of the Interview

July 11, 2002

"Forty-five years have come and gone since then, Mr. Pentak," declared Theodore McBride, turning from his fortieth-floor window, "and I've tried to live up to that promise every day since. The first day I came here I made the decision to invest myself in my people. The sight of the neglected flock I had seen with Jack Neumann remained vivid in my memory." McBride looked my way, then said, "I decided I wasn't going to let that happen on *my* watch. As implausible as it may sound, I did just what Jack taught me on those Texas hillsides. Over the years, with few exceptions, my people have responded just like he said they would."

"I should think the results speak for themselves," I said.

"Well," he replied, "we've been able to recruit the best people in the world to come work here. What's more, our flock hasn't fallen for the greener-grass syndrome. The list of people trying to get into General Technologies is far greater than the list of people trying to get out. Our people *want* to work here. As a result, GT has one of the highest retention rates of any Fortune 50 company in America."

"That seems to be pretty important to you," I said as I took notes.

"Oh, absolutely," McBride answered. "And it illustrates how Neumann was so far ahead of his time. Back in 1957 we lived in a manufacturing economy. The marketplace was about assembly lines and standardization. People weren't as concerned about quality-of-life issues then. But today we live in a service economy and an information age. It's all about processes and customization. As a result, many of the assets a company has are intellectual in nature."

"I'm sorry, what does that mean?" I asked.

"It means that a company's competitive advantage is comprised of the skills and knowledge of its people."

"In other words, their know-how," I suggested.

"Yes," McBride replied. "And since people today *are* concerned about quality-of-life issues, they're careful about choosing which pasture they will graze in. So a key to maintaining your competitive advantage is to retain your talent."

"I think I get it," I said. "'General Technologies: Our People Are Our Greatest Competitive Advantage.'"

McBride smiled at me. "I'm beginning to think I made a wise selection in choosing you for the interview," he said.

"Thank you," I replied, sitting a little taller in my chair. "I appreciate the compliment. There is one thing I'm not sure I understand, though."

"What's that, Bill?" McBride asked.

"You said that Neumann was ahead of his time."

"Yes, he was."

"But even he taught you that shepherds have been leading their flocks for thousands of years."

"Oh, I understand your confusion," McBride said. "What you want to know is how could something as ancient as the Way of the Shepherd still work today?"

"Yes," I said. "And why don't we have more shepherd-leaders like you?"

"The principles of the Way of the Shepherd still work after thousands of years because the basic needs of people have remained essentially the same," he explained. "As to why more people don't shepherd their people, Jack answered that himself. Great leadership comes at a price that too few are willing to pay."

"So whatever happened to Dr. Neumann?" I asked.

"He passed on years ago," McBride said. "He's long gone but not forgotten." At that, McBride walked from the window over to the wall opposite his desk. I turned and saw that he was standing next to two sticks mounted on the wall. One was long; the other, short. McBride ran his hand along the long stick that had a large curve near the top.

"He left these to me in his will," he said. "I've missed him a great deal. I've been blessed with the many accolades that adorn these walls, Mr. Pentak—more than a person *ought* to have—but none of them mean more to me than these two. Jack Neumann left his mark on me. I owe much of my success to him, for teaching me the greatest management secrets in the world. He taught me how to instill loyalty and commitment in my people. He taught me how to lead people in a manner that made them want to follow. There isn't a week that goes by that I don't think of him."

He slowly walked back toward his desk and continued. "I think he would be proud of what we've done here. At the very least, I think he would feel he earned a good return on his investment in me."

"What more could you possibly do?" I said.

"I can spread the word," he said, taking his chair. "I can teach other young students what he taught me."

"So that's why you agreed to do the interview," I said. "You want to spread the word."

"Now you know," McBride said, softly chuckling. "It's also the reason my company will be sending out a press release tomorrow announcing my retirement, pending the selection of my successor."

I sat bolt upright for a moment, then flipped the page on my notepad. "Can you tell me who your replacement will be?" I asked nervously.

"That's another interview, another day," McBride replied shrewdly. "I can tell you that my successor won't be a hireling or a stranger. I'm not turning my flock over to anyone but the best shepherd I know."

"What do you think will happen here when you leave?" I asked. "Are you worried in any way that GT will slip?"

"Not at all. I've already told you that we have the best and the brightest working here. I've also spent forty-five years telling the General Technologies family what we're about. These people won't stand for the bar to be lowered. They're too committed to the GT Way."

"You mean, the Way of the Shepherd?" I asked.

McBride smiled. "Yes, the Way of the Shepherd."

Just then, Christina Nickel's voice came over McBride's intercom.

"Mr. McBride, your phone conference with the dean is in ten minutes," she said.

"Thank you, Christina." He turned to me and thrust his hand across the table. "Thank you for coming today," he said. "I appreciate the time you've given me, and I look forward to reading what you write."

"Thank you," I said, shaking his hand. "Thank you for giving me such an opportunity. I will do my very best."

"I know you will," McBride said. "Good-bye."

By the time I rose from my seat, Christina Nickel was already standing in the doorway to escort me to the elevator. No sooner had we left McBride's office than Christina's phone rang. While she ran to grab her line, I took the opportunity to look back through the cracked door at the remarkable Theodore McBride. He sat behind his immense desk, staring across the room, and forty-five years of his life, to the staff and *knobkerrie* on the wall. "Thank you, Jack," I saw him whisper, "I couldn't have done it without you."

For several long moments McBride sat there alone, his mind awash in the memories of another time and place. After a while, a small smile crept across his face as he reached toward the lower left-hand drawer of his immense desk. Reaching in, he pulled an old, tattered notepad out of the drawer and laid it on his desk. Cracking the well-worn cover, he opened to the notebook's first page. There, scribbled in fading ink on yellowed paper, were the words "The Way of the Shepherd."

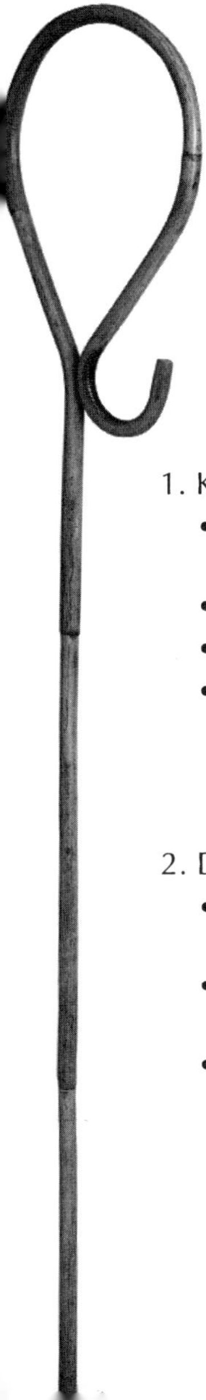

Principles of the Way of the Shepherd

1. Know the Condition of Your Flock
   - Follow the status of your people as well as the status of the work.
   - Get to know your flock, one sheep at a time.
   - Engage your people on a regular basis.
   - Keep your eyes and ears open, question, and follow through.

2. Discover the Shape of Your Sheep
   - Your choice of sheep can make flock management easier or harder.
   - Start with healthy sheep, or you'll inherit someone else's problems.
   - Know the SHAPE of your sheep to make sure they're in the right fold.

3. Help Your Sheep Identify with You
    - Build trust with your followers by modeling authenticity, integrity, and compassion.
    - Set high standards of performance.
    - Relentlessly communicate your values and sense of mission.
    - Define the cause for your people and tell them where they fit in.
    - Remember that great leadership isn't just professional; it's personal.

4. Make Your Pasture a Safe Place
    - Keep your people well informed.
    - Infuse *every* position with importance.
    - Cull chronic instigators from the flock.
    - Regularly rotate the sheep to fresh pastures.
    - Reassure the sheep by staying visible.
    - Don't give problems time to fester.

5. The Staff of Direction
   - Know where you're going, get out in front, and keep your flock on the move.
   - When directing, use persuasion rather than coercion.
   - Give your people freedom of movement, but make sure they know where the fence line is. Don't confuse boundaries with bridles!
   - When your people get in trouble, go and get them out.
   - Remind your people that failure isn't fatal.

6. The Rod of Correction
   - *Protect:* Stand in the gap and fight for your sheep.
   - *Correct:* Approach discipline as a teaching opportunity.
   - *Inspect:* Regularly inquire about your people's progress.

7. The Heart of the Shepherd
   - Great leadership is a lifestyle, not a technique.
   - Every day you have to decide who's going to pay for your leadership—you or your people.
   - Most of all, have a heart for your sheep.

In all your ways acknowledge Him . . .

Notes

Chapter 2. Discover the Shape of Your Sheep

1. Barbara Smith, Mark Aseltine, and Gerald Kennedy, *Beginning Shepherd's Manual*, 2d ed. (Ames, Iowa: Iowa State University Press, 1997), 19.
2. Adapted from Rick Warren, "When You Say Someone Is SHAPED for Ministry, What Do You Mean?" *Rick Warren's Ministry Toolbox* no. 52 (22 March 2002), 1.
3. From Phillip Keller, *A Shepherd Looks at Psalm 23* (Grand Rapids: Zondervan, 1970), 32.

Chapter 3. Help Your Sheep Identify with You

1. Ibid., 23.

Chapter 4. Make Your Pasture a Safe Place

1. This term was coined by Adam Brandenburger of Harvard Business School and Barry Nalebuff of the Yale School of Management. It is the title of a book they published with Doubleday in 1996.
2. Keller, *A Shepherd Looks at Psalm 23*, 28.
3. Ibid., 35.
4. Ibid., 44.

Chapter 5. The Staff of Direction

1. Smith, Aseltine, and Kennedy, *Beginning Shepherd's Manual*, 8.
2. Larry Pierce, *The New John Gill Exposition of the Entire Bible, Modernised and Adapted for the Computer* (Winterbourne, Ontario: Online Bible), http://www.studylight.org/com/geb.
3. M. G. Easton, *Illustrated Bible Dictionary*, 3d ed. (Thomas Nelson, 1897). Public domain; copy freely.
4. Smith, Aseltine, and Kennedy, *Beginning Shepherd's Manual*, 73.
5. Donald T. Phillips, *Lincoln on Leadership: Executive Strategies for Tough Times* (New York: Warner, 1993), 38.
6. Adapted from Keller, *A Shepherd Looks at Psalm 23*, 103.
7. Jack Welch and John A. Byrne, *Jack: Straight from the Gut* (New York: Warner Business, 2001), 29.

Chapter 6. The Rod of Correction

1. Fred H. Wright, *Manners and Customs of Bible Lands* (Chicago: Moody Press, 1953), 149.
2. Keller, *A Shepherd Looks at Psalm 23*, 95.

Chapter 7. The Heart of the Shepherd

1. Wright, *Manners and Customs of Bible Lands*, 157. (See also John 10:3.)
2. Ibid, 155.
3. Ibid.

Selected Bibliography

Easton, M. G. *Illustrated Bible Dictionary*. 3d ed. Nashville: Thomas Nelson, 1897.

Keller, Phillip. *A Shepherd Looks at Psalm 23*. Grand Rapids: Zondervan, 1970.

Phillips, Donald T. *Lincoln on Leadership: Executive Strategies for Tough Times*. New York: Warner, 1993.

Smith, Barbara, Mark Aseltine, and Gerald Kennedy. *Beginning Shepherd's Manual*. 2d ed. Ames, IA: Iowa State University Press, 1997.

Warren, Rick. "When You Say Someone Is SHAPED for Ministry, What Do You Mean?" *Rick Warren's Ministry Tool Box* no. 52 (22 May 2002).

Wright, Fred H. *Manners and Customs of Bible Lands*. Chicago: Moody Press, 1953.

For information regarding speaking availability, business consultations, or seminars, please contact Bill Pentak at:

Bill Pentak
P.O. Box 203
Cypress, TX 77410-0203
Phone (713) 559-1139
Website www.billpentak.com

For information regarding speaking availability, business consultations, or seminars, please contact Dr. Leman at:

Dr. Kevin Leman
P.O. Box 35370
Tucson, Arizona 85740
Phone (520) 797-3830
Fax (520) 797-3809
Websites:
www.realfamilies.com
www.matchwise.com
www.drleman.com

Books by Dr. Kevin Leman

Winning the Rat Race without Becoming a Rat
The Birth Order Book
Making Children Mind without Losing Yours
First Time Mom
A Chicken's Guide to Talking Turkey with Your Kids about Sex
The Way of the Shepherd
Sex Begins in the Kitchen
The Perfect Match
Sheet Music—Uncovering the Secrets of Sexual Intimacy in Marriage
When Your Best Is Not Good Enough
Women Who Try Too Hard
Becoming the Parent God Wants You to Be
Becoming a Couple of Promise
Living in a Stepfamily without Getting Stepped On
What a Difference a Daddy Makes
Making Sense of the Men in Your Life
Say Goodbye to Stress
The Real You—Becoming the Person You Were Meant to Be
Unlocking the Secrets of Your Childhood Memories
Keeping Your Family Strong in a World Gone Wrong
Ten Secrets to Raising Sensible, Successful Kids
My Firstborn, There's No One Like You
My Middle Child, There's No One Like You
My Lastborn, There's No One Like You
My Only Child, There's No One Like You

Audiotapes

Why Kids Misbehave and What You Can Do about It
How to Make Your Child Feel Special
Keeping Your Family Together When the World Is Falling Apart
Living in a Stepfamily without Getting Stepped On

Videotapes

Raising Successful and Confident Kids
How to Get Kids to Do What You Want
Why Kids Misbehave and What You Can Do about It
Living in a Stepfamily without Getting Stepped On

Video Series (with study guide, DVD, and audiotape)

Making Children Mind without Losing Yours (Christian parenting edition)
Making Children Mind without Losing Yours (public-school edition)
Making the Most of Marriage
Single Parenting That Works!
Bringing Peace and Harmony to the Blended Family

Dr. Kevin Leman

"Practical Wisdom with a Smile"

Founder of www.matchwise.com, internationally known Christian psychologist, award-winning author, radio and television personality, and speaker, Dr. Kevin Leman has ministered to and entertained audiences worldwide with his wit and common-sense psychology.

Bestselling author Dr. Leman has made house calls for Focus on the Family with Dr. James Dobson, as well as numerous radio and television programs including, *Oprah*, *Live with Regis and Kelly*, CBS's *The Early Show*, *Today*, and *The View with Barbara Walters*. Dr. Leman is a frequent contributor to CNN's *American Morning*. Dr. Leman has served as a consulting family psychologist to *Good Morning America*.

Dr. Leman is founder and president of Couples of Promise, an organization designed for and committed to helping couples remain happily married.

Dr. Leman's professional affiliations include the American Psychological Association, American Federation of Radio and

Television Artists, National Register of Health Services Providers in Psychology, and the North American Society of Adlerian Psychology.

Dr. Leman attended North Park College. He received his bachelor's degree in psychology from the University of Arizona, where he later earned his master's and doctorate degrees. Originally from Williamsville, New York, he and his wife, Sande, live in Tucson. They have five children and one grandchild.

PURSUE SIGNIFICANCE, ACHIEVE TOP PERFORMANCE

From Success to Significance

When the Pursuit of Success Isn't Enough

Lloyd Reeb unfolds a blueprint that has helped thousands of men and women redefine success and infuse their lives with eternal significance. Adapt Reeb's approach to your circumstances and, with God's help, put it in motion. It works, and it will work for you.

Top Performance

How to Develop Excellence in Yourself and Others

These dynamic principles developed by master salesman Zig Ziglar are applicable to the office, home, sports, church, or other organizations. Sprinkled with Ziglar's wit and helpful illustrations, they'll propel you—and those around you—toward Top Performance.

11/3K/3.2009/EC